# Praise for *Nonprofit Program Evaluation Made Simple*

*Chari demonstrates a keen understanding of how important evaluation is to nonprofit work. She lays it out clearly with an easy-to-read style that makes evaluation understandable to nonprofits seeking to implement sound evaluation processes.*

—Mark R. McCrary, Program Coordinator, Grantmakers of Oregon and SW Washington

*This book is perfect for nonprofits who are either not collecting performance data, or not using what they have effectively. Chari Smith has written an essential guide for nonprofits, packed with numerous real-life examples and a ton of practical, straightforward advice to motivate staff at every level in this area.*

—Kylie Hutchinson, author of *A Short Primer on Innovative Evaluation Reporting*

*Making the complex simple, the complicated doable, the abstract concrete, and the frightening friendly takes a special combination of expertise, experience, and communications skill. Chari Smith brings all that and more to this accessible, important, and insightful book. She shows how to design evaluations that are useful, focus on what's important, and turn findings into actions. Nonprofits will profit enormously from the step-by-step guidance that moves from preparation and planning through question formulation and data collection to making sense of and applying findings. This book delivers on its title. Read, learn, and engage.*

—Michael Quinn Patton, CEO and author, Utilization-Focused Evaluation

*The ability to measure impact and share that success with the world is foundational to a thriving nonprofit and unlock doors leading to visibility and funding. Leaders mistakenly believe that the process is too expensive, too timing consuming or that their kind of work can't be measured. Chari's approach to program evaluation will bust these myths and unlock these doors—offering a simple and accessible approach to your efforts to invite more people to know more and do more for your cause.*

–Joan Garry, Author of Nonprofits are Messy,
Principal at Joan Garry Consulting and
Founder of Nonprofit Leadership Lab

*This book provides an excellent blueprint for nonprofits to follow as Smith outlines all the necessary steps to get from the idea phase of evaluation to creating reports and communicating the data in a way that shows impact of your program(s) that stakeholders, community members and funders will all understand and appreciate. I found Chapter 4 (Build A Culture of Evaluation) important as I have learned from her that evaluation is not done in a silo and this chapter specifically addresses how to build an organizational culture that will support all parts of the evaluation process.*

–Jean Hansen, Vice President, School Partnerships and
Youth Outreach, Special Olympics Oregon

*Understanding your organization's impact requires using data to learn and improve on a regular basis and that can be a daunting task. In this book, Chari Smith has demystified the process of creating an effective evaluation process for nonprofits. The book offers many practical tips that will help your organization improve results.*

–Beth Kanter, Virtual Facilitator, Trainer, and Author
(www.bethkanter.org)

*The evaluation design and monitoring for a program is something that I find often feels like a process that is overwhelming for staff resources or requires external support. However, with the steps and templates in this book as a reference, I believe any grant team (which I define as a group of colleagues with a stake in grants being successful) can approach evaluation design in a way that strengthens their grant applications and decreases the stress of their grant implementation and management.*

–Diane H. Leonard, GPC, President/Owner/Trainer
DH Leonard Consulting and Grant Writing Services, LLC

*Chari Smith has written a comprehensive guide to do-it-yourself evaluation. She's realistic about what nonprofits are getting themselves into, providing expert advice clearly grounded in years of experience. Evaluation IS a large undertaking—and one that will change an organization's culture for the better. Chari breaks down the steps of the process and makes it feel accomplishable. The many success stories from nonprofit leaders throughout the book testify that evaluation doesn't have to be intimidating and can, in fact, help change the world.*

–Stephanie Evergreen, Author of three data visualization
books and Founder of Evergreen Data Visualization Academy

*The data helped us secure two of our largest grants to date. Even though increasing our grant funding was the primary reason we started this process, the real success is our ongoing ability to gather data that are relevant to our work and using it to continually improve our program.*

–Julia Doty, Program Director, NW Housing Alternatives

*Because of having this program evaluation system in place, our annual fundraising from foundations increased by 677 percent and annual fundraising from individual donors increased by 753 percent.*

–Brandi Tuck, Executive Director,
Portland Homeless Family Solutions

# NONPROFIT

## PROGRAM EVALUATION

## MADE SIMPLE

### GET YOUR DATA.
### SHOW YOUR IMPACT.
### IMPROVE YOUR PROGRAMS.

# NONPROFIT
## PROGRAM EVALUATION
## MADE SIMPLE

### GET YOUR DATA.
### SHOW YOUR IMPACT.
### IMPROVE YOUR PROGRAMS.

CHARI SMITH

# Nonprofit Program Evaluation Made Simple
By Chari Smith

Chari Smith is the President and Founder of Evaluation into Action, providing a range of services such as creating your program evaluation plan, helping you to implement it, training, coaching, and more. Learn more at www.evaluationintoaction.com.

A project of Author Brick Road™, a Division of CharityChannel LLC
Manuscript editing: Carol Carmick, Standing Wave of Portland, Oregon
Cover design: JD&J Design LLC
Interior design and layout: Stephen C. Nill, Author Brick Road

Published by Chari Smith
Copyright © 2020 Chari Smith

ISBN: 978-0-578-80388-3
Library of Congress Control Number: 2020922496
13 12 11 10 9 8 7 6 5 4 3 2 1

A Project of

Author Brick Road, a division of CharityChannel, leverages
its deep publishing experience to empower visionary
and transformative leaders to write and publish books of
extraordinary impact, clarity, and usefulness.

# Dedication

For my dad, the late Dr. Harvey Greenberg, who told me I can do anything. He always said, "Do what you love to do and you'll never work a day in your life." For my husband, Tom, who is supportive regardless of my whimsical ideas and neurotic drive. For my boys, Miles and Max, who inspire me every day.

# Acknowledgments

I first want to acknowledge the workshop participants who approached me to ask for a book. I thank you for your interest in this approach and the encouragement to write it all down.

Many clients generously shared their experiences and gave permission for our work to be included in this book. I sincerely appreciate their willingness to share these critical examples of program evaluation work. Thanks to Julia Doty, Brandi Tuck, Michael Parkhurst, Jean Hansen, Elaine Philippi Charpentier, Jackie Groah, Justin Yuen, and Ariela Friedman.

A special thank you to fellow evaluator Kylie Hutchinson for permission to excerpt her book. I worked with Kelly Jarvis at NPC Research on a project funded by the Oregon Arts Commission, where we developed six evaluation mini-guides for a project titled "Connecting Students to the World of Work." Special thanks to Deb Vaughn, Oregon Arts Commission Director, for permission to excerpt those guides.

I am grateful to Amanda Jarman and Jerian Abel for reviewing drafts even before they went to the publisher. Your valuable feedback helped shape this book.

Thanks to Dr. Michael Quinn Patton and Dr. Stephanie Evergreen, whose work inspired me to push beyond what I thought was possible in the field of program evaluation. To Agnes Zach, who helped my program evaluation practice grow. And to long-time members of my Evaluation into Action team: Research Associate Christine Chvatal, who is a master project juggler, and Robyn Barbon with Folklore Media, who is a graphic design magician.

With much gratitude, I thank my husband Tom and boys Miles and Max, who have been supportive throughout this writing journey. Thanks for advocating that I take the plunge and write this book. And thanks to my good friends JoAnn and Todd Watson for the use of their dining room table for many mini writing retreats while they were away at work.

Thanks to Stephen Nill with CharityChannel's Author Brick Road division for his ongoing support and dedication to making this book the best it can possibly be.

And thanks to you, reader, for taking the time to dive in and learn how to get and use your data. I hope you enjoy your program evaluation journey!

# Contents

## Part Four: Create Your Reports

# Foreword

**M**y first reaction when reading this book was, "Wow! Chari has put into easy-to-understand language what has taken me years to learn." *Nonprofit Program Evaluation Made Simple* is filled with concepts that I used during my thirty years as a program developer, fundraiser, and executive director that helped me be successful. And it can help you too.

Evaluation is essential to nonprofit growth. You need to conduct evaluation to know where you are, benchmark your performance, and move your organization forward. By reading this book, you learn from an expert, as Chari tells you how to plan for, allocate resources to, set goals, get buy-in, and conduct evaluation so that you reach your destination.

Evaluative data helps inform program design. For example, it can shape the methods you consider to best reach your intended client outcomes. In addition, data collection techniques can easily be folded into client intake and exit forms. Chari gives you plenty of examples of how to do this—guidance I wish I had as a program developer.

Objective data helps you present an accurate picture of what is going on in your community and measure your agency's impact. As such, logic or impact models are often required by funders when submitting a proposal, particularly for larger requests. Chari shows you exactly how to develop your own logic and impact models. And how to use them beyond proposal submission.

As you try to be noticed in the crowd and heard above the fray, your nonprofit must present a strong, consistent image of success. If you project one semblance and are subsequently revealed as a fake, you are done for, unable to attract the community support you need to fulfill your mission. Objective data establishes your nonprofit's credibility. And helps you rebuff your detractors.

Chari tells you step by step how to create an effective evaluation system and manage organizational culture to embrace it. She conveys how to solve project management issues. She even compares spreadsheet versus database management systems and gives you tips on selecting vendors.

Fear not! Nonprofit program assessment, skillfully presented by Chari, makes evaluation easy.

Joanne Oppelt, MHA

Joanne Oppelt Consulting LLC

# Introduction

Let's say that you're completing a grant application that includes this question: *How will you evaluate your project?* It used to be enough to say that you plan to evaluate your project by tracking the number of service hours delivered and the people who participated.

Not anymore.

Funders want to know what difference your organization makes. Meeting this demand opens the door to integrating program evaluation into your organization's daily operations—so that when funders need data on a project or program, you already have an organization-wide system in place to fulfill those requests.

The entry point to the evaluation process often stems from grant writers needing data. But once the process begins, it soon becomes clear that regularly gathering and reporting data both promotes continuous program improvement *and* demonstrates your organization's positive impact.

The culture shifts from chasing data for each funder request to using data to learn. A very different mindset—and a much less stressful one!

I am passionate about program evaluation as a learning opportunity. Resistance to program evaluation typically stems from not understanding what it is, why to do it, and how to do it.

This book addresses these questions. It outlines how to create a program evaluation process for your organization. It's for anyone who wants to:

- Learn the basics of nonprofit program evaluation
- Understand how to build buy-in for evaluation
- Create a realistic and meaningful system for program evaluation
- Identify measurable outcomes and a logic model for a program
- Create basic data collection tools like surveys
- Understand how to manage program data in a user-friendly way
- Generate reports to inform program design
- Leverage data to support development efforts

This book provides step-by-step directions from the beginning of the evaluation process to the end. It blends both process and outcome evaluation, giving you data to improve program implementation and demonstrate overall impact.

Some portions of this book are basic, while others are more in-depth. Feel free to read cover to cover, jump to a section, or skip around as needed.

## Companion Website

This book has a companion website to support your program evaluation process: www.evaluationintoaction.com/getyourdata.

Enter the password *useyourdata* and your email address.

Throughout this book, this icon ⌨ means there's more information on the website.

The companion website includes the following documents. Please note, the companion website will be updated regularly, so check back periodically.

**Impact Models.** As described in Part Two, impact models are an alternative to logic models. They align with your brand and answer the questions: 1. What does your program do? and 2. What difference do you expect it to make?

1. Candlelighters for Children with Cancer Family Camp impact model
2. Northwest Housing Alternatives Resident Services Program impact model
3. In4All: STEM™ Connect impact model
4. Portland Homeless Family Solutions: Shelter Program impact model

**Timelines.** These are a critical part of your program evaluation plan. Here are two examples of timelines to help you create your own:

5. Northwest Housing Alternatives NHA timeline
6. In4All timeline

**Database Architecture.** This document defines data to be collected and what users need to get out of the database.

7. Northwest Housing Alternatives Resident Services Program database architecture overview

**Survey design template.** Refer to Chapter 13 on survey design to use this template to create your own survey.

8. Survey design template

**Permission form.** This is the same permission form in Chapter 13, an editable version so you can modify it for your own use.

9. Permission form

**Reports.** A summary report is a user-friendly document you can share with the public at large. Learn from these examples on how to use graphics and layout techniques to make your report visually appealing.

10. Portland Homeless Family Solutions Annual report

11. Candlelighters for Children with Cancer Program Impact summary report

12. Northwest Housing Alternatives Resident Services program impact summary report

13. Meyer Memorial Trust: Affordable Housing Initiative Manufactured Home Repair program summary report

## Part One

# GET READY

Program evaluation is a learning tool. The key reason to do program evaluation is to learn what is going well and where improvements are needed.

Everyday life has situations where evaluation is required. For instance, imagine that an Olympic swimmer in training is never timed. They may feel like they're swimming fast, and people might say, "You swim really fast!" but that's all anecdotal evidence. Unless they know their times, how can they know how much faster they need to be to win?

Or imagine a middle school student who's taking classes in social studies, math, literature, and science, but they never receive grades. Teachers tell them they're a great student, and they take tests but don't receive scores—just a pat on the back. How will anyone know if they've learned what they're supposed to?

These situations show the need for athletes and students to evaluate their performance to improve. The same holds true for nonprofit organizations. Program evaluation gathers data to answer important questions so people in your organization can be sure they are making the difference they intend.

Joan Garry, founder of the Nonprofit Leadership Lab and author of *Nonprofits are Messy*, identifies fourteen attributes of a thriving nonprofit in her blog. The eighth one focuses on program evaluation:

> *Programs are evaluated to determine impact. It's not enough to simply have anecdotes of impact. The best nonprofit organizations have mechanisms in place to measure success. It's key to strategic planning, and yes, funders want to know too.*

I couldn't agree with this sentiment more. Too often, nonprofits feel the stories their participants tell them is enough. It's not. To truly measure success, you need a systematic way to gather data that will clearly demonstrate the impact you're making.

As Joan says, funders want to know the impact your program makes. Funders also want to know about the challenges as well as successes. As Michael Parkhurst, Program Officer for the Meyer Memorial Trust, says:

> *It can tell a powerful story about how your program is making a big difference for the people you are trying to help. The flipside is accountability. If you're not measuring anything, then you're not holding yourself accountable. Data that shows you're NOT meeting your targets is telling you something important!*

When done right, program evaluation fuels fundraising efforts. Most grant proposals require that forecast of what measurable outcomes your program will have, and then the report on those outcomes once the program is complete. Being able to demonstrate impact in a meaningful way catalyzes support from potential donors, foundations, and other funding sources.

Brandi Tuck, Executive Director with Portland Homeless Family Solutions, saw dramatic fundraising results through program evaluation:

> *Because of having this program evaluation system in place, our annual fundraising from foundations increased by 677 percent and annual fundraising from individual donors increased by 753 percent.*

When she shared this, it nearly knocked me off my seat! Now, I still hold that the real reason to do program evaluation is for continuous program improvement. But this example of turning data into dollars is worth noting.

The following chapter provides an overview of what program evaluation is.

# CHAPTER 1

# What is Program Evaluation?

*I* knew we needed better data for our resident services program. I knew the work we were doing was making a difference. We had no formal structures in place to show our impact. We had difficulty communicating to grant funders the impact of our work. Funders didn't understand what we were doing and why we were doing it. The data we were collecting weren't effective.

*The thought of doing program evaluation seemed like an overwhelming process. Some staff were resistant to the concept. I just didn't know where to start.*

*In 2016, we contracted with Chari Smith, President/Founder of Evaluation into Action (EIA), to create an evaluation system for our program. This six-month process resulted in an increased ability to effectively communicate our impact, what our services are, and why we are offering them.*

*In fact, the data helped us secure two of our largest grants to date. Even though increasing our grant funding was the primary reason we started this process, the real success is our ongoing ability to gather data that are relevant to our work and use them to continually improve our program. In fact, we have been able to use these data to continually improve our program and offer more effective interventions, allowing us to package our work so that funders can clearly understand our program goals and impact.*

*In the beginning, I thought this was going to be hard. It wasn't. The whole process was broken down into manageable steps, helping us to understand how to do program evaluation on our own. I am excited that examples from our program evaluation process are included in this book. Believe me, I know program evaluation can feel overwhelming, but it's not. It's one of the most valuable investments we've made.*

**—Julia Doty, Program Director, NW Housing Alternatives**

Working with Julia's team is just one example of how program evaluation can be integrated into your day-to-day operations. This book provides step-by-step guidance on how to do program evaluation. It makes it easy for you to get the data you need to improve your programs as well as show your impact.

Okay, you know you need to do program evaluation. So, what exactly is it? Kylie Hutchinson's book, *Survive and Thrive: Three Steps to Securing Your Program's Sustainability*, includes this great explanation:

Each program is unique, but our fundamental principles for establishing a useful program evaluation process are the same:

## Excerpt: Demonstrating Your Worth

***Evaluation 101***

***A Primer on Demonstrating Your Worth***

*Many of you will already be familiar with the term program evaluation. Here's a popular definition from Dr. Michael Quinn Patton's book,* Essentials of Utilization-Focused Evaluation:

*Program evaluation is the systematic collection and analysis of information about program activities, characteristics, and outcomes to make judgments about the program, improve program effectiveness, and/or inform decisions about future programming.*

*Below is a simple overview of the two most common types of evaluation.*

### Process Evaluation

*A process evaluation (also called formative evaluation) focuses on how your program is being implemented and operates. It ensures that your program remains on track to achieve later outcomes. A process evaluation answers questions such as:*

- *Are we providing services as intended?*
- *What is working well and not working well with our services?*
- *Are we reaching our target market?*
- *Are participants satisfied with the program?*
- *What else could or should we be doing?*

### Outcome Evaluation

*An outcome evaluation (also called summative evaluation) determines what outcomes and impacts have occurred as a result of your program. Outcomes are benefits or changes as a result of your program's activities. It answers questions such as:*

- *Was the program effective?*
- *What difference did it make?*
- *Do our outcomes differ across different sites?*
- *Was it worth it given the overall time and resources invested?*

Use a collaborative and inclusive process to define what you are measuring; measure it; then use the results.

Other evaluation methods are complex, requiring statistical analysis, randomized trials, and other methods requiring trained professionals.

Our approach here is based on the premise that you and your organization can build a culture of evaluation, collaboratively define measurable outcomes, create a plan, collect data, and report on and use the results.

Methods for gathering data include basic surveys coupled with stories from participants. This mixed-methods approach combines quantitative (numbers) and qualitative (stories) data to provide a comprehensive picture of how the program is fulfilling its outcomes.

# CHAPTER 2

# Understand the Terminology

Program evaluation includes a lot of terms that are used inter-changeably by evaluators, funders, and nonprofit professionals. This can cause confusion about the meanings of terms like objective versus goal.

In this book, we use the terms listed below. A lot. Get comfort-able with them, and don't worry if you've heard them used differently elsewhere. That is totally OK. There's a lack of common language in the field, and it's just fine as long as we're clear on how we're using them here.

- **Goal:** The big broad vision for your program.
- **Methodology:** How data are collected through methods such as surveys, focus groups, interviews, etc.
- **Measurement:** A specific data collection tool, like "Parent Survey" or "intake form."
    - → **Methodology vs. measurement:** Methodology is a

general approach to how data are collected. Measurement is a data collection tool used for a specific purpose.

- **Output:** This is "bean counting": measuring how many people participated in an event, how many people participated in your program, and so on.
- **Outcome:** This is a change statement. What do you expect to change as a result of program activities? Outcomes are generally expressed in terms of changes to knowledge, skills, attitude, and/or behavior.
  - → Output vs. outcome: Outputs measure simple metrics like the number of participants, hours, and so on. Outcomes measure change and are generally more complex.
- **Input:** Resources for your program, such as staff, partner, space, equipment, etc.
- **Data:** The term "data" is plural, and is used that way throughout this book.

All of these terms are described in more detail in the following pages. By understanding these basic program evaluation terms, you will be on your way to wearing the program evaluation hat.

# CHAPTER 3

# Plan Your Resources

It's essential to plan your resources before creating an evaluation process. Too often, people jump into creating a survey with no resource planning, then later realize no one is available to analyze the data. Or they embark on a two-year project and in the last month reach out to evaluators: "I have a two-year project that needs a summative evaluation. The final report is due in a month, and we have $3,000 to hire someone."

This is all too common—and completely unrealistic. Not planning your resources results in inadequate time, expertise, and funds to properly conduct program evaluation. An evaluation plan needs to be in place before implementing the program. Ideally, program and evaluation planning occur concurrently.

Here are some guidelines to help with resource planning:

## Time

A common reason for not doing program evaluation is lack of time. It's true: program evaluation takes time. But the return on your investment is understanding more about your program: what's working, what needs improvement, and what is its overall impact? Initially, the design phase takes the most time, but once evaluation activities are integrated into program implementation, they become part of your day-to-day work.

## Costs

A common guideline for the cost of the evaluation is 10 to 15 percent of the total program budget. This may include doing all the work internally, retaining an external evaluator, or some combination. For example, an external evaluator can help develop the evaluation plan, while the internal staff may implement it.

Cost varies depending upon what methodology you choose to employ. Surveys tend to be less expensive than focus groups. It also depends on how much expertise and time is available from staff members versus hiring an outside consultant.

*Table: Budget strategies*

| Plan on 10 to 15% of program budget for evaluation, either by internal staff, external consultants, or a blend | | |
|---|---|---|
| **Internal** | **Blend** | **External** |
| Evaluation is done entirely by staff members | Use a consultant to help design the evaluation plan, create data collection tools, and/or complete evaluation report | Evaluation is done completely by an outside firm |

As Theresa Deussen and Kari Nelsestuen explain in their booklet, *Being a Savvy Consumer of Evaluation:*

*The amount of money needed for an evaluation depends on a variety of factors, including what aspects of your program you decide to evaluate, the size of the program, the number of outcomes you want to assess, who conducts the evaluation, and your nonprofit's available evaluation-related resources. Costs can also vary depending upon your communities and geographic location.*

Here are some typical evaluation activities at the lowest, moderate, and highest cost levels. These are adapted from Deussen and Nelsestuen's booklet.

**Lowest cost.** A less expensive evaluation will likely include monitoring the number of participants, number of services, and other "bean counting" activities (also called *outputs*). You want to have the system for this in place before measuring outcomes. Outputs require a systematic approach to ensure these data are regularly captured in a standardized way. We will address how to accomplish this in Part Three: Collect Your Data.

**Moderate cost.** This level includes the activities listed above as well as creating an evaluation framework that defines measurable outcomes in terms of changes in knowledge, behaviors, attitudes, or skills. A survey is a less expensive data collection method, often used to gather data to inform to what degree outcomes were achieved. This book uses the moderate cost approach, ensuring a basic evaluation framework, which serves as the foundation for other evaluation activities.

**Highest cost.** Data collection activities will likely include a combination of two or more of the following: surveys, focus groups, on-site visits, and observations. Comparison—or using a control group—tends to be the most expensive, requiring outside expertise. Sometimes organizations receive a grant specifically to do an in-depth study in affiliation with a university or third-party evaluator. These studies are valuable and provide a unique opportunity to measure impact. However, they are often resource-intensive in terms of cost, time, and expertise. If you want this type of evaluation, plan on hiring an outside expert.

A program evaluation in the moderate cost range allows you to gather output and outcome data in a realistic and meaningful way.

Both formative and summative evaluation can be achieved concurrently in the moderate cost range if an evaluation is designed to be both meaningful and realistic. Formative evaluation measures ongoing program effectiveness and is truly an organizational development tool. A summative evaluation reports at a program's conclusion (or at a break in an ongoing program cycle) and generally measures impact. For more on this, see Part Two: Create Your Plan.

## Expertise

Some evaluation approaches require professional training or education. The approach in this book requires an understanding of what program evaluation is and a willingness to learn how to create a process that is both realistic and meaningful. Basic data collection, management, analysis, and reporting are detailed in later chapters.

The key is to put one person at the helm of driving the evaluation process, from planning to implementation to using the results.

## Questions to Consider

- **Expertise:** Is there someone on staff, preferably the program director, who has experience with program evaluation?

  A common arrangement is for the program director to oversee the evaluation process and a program coordinator to handle day-to-day project management to implement the evaluation.

- **Time:** Can you set aside two to three months to collaboratively design your program evaluation process?

  Once the plan is set, it is a matter of assigning a compulsively organized person to oversee the implementation of the plan.

  The time this will take depends on whether you're doing evaluation internally, using an external consultant, or a combination. If you're doing it internally, plan on having a committee of two to four people run the project. They will likely need to spend five to 10 hours per week in the planning phase, with a project manager to oversee ongoing implementation.

  If you hire an outside consultant, they will spend most of their time on developing the plan and process. Staff will likely need to participate in surveys, meetings, and other ways of providing input on the plan.

- **Money:** What funds can you regularly allocate toward program evaluation?

  If you're on the lower end of the cost spectrum, be prepared to stay within your budget, which may mean doing less initially than planned. It is important to start small, be successful, and then expand your evaluation system.

You need to commit resources to ensure success. The investment is worth it! Don't just take my word for it. Director of Resident Services for Northwest Housing Alternatives, Julia Doty, shares her experience:

> *Our program evaluation process saves us time and money by allowing our team to assess what services are most and least utilized as well as which services are most impactful. Program evaluation informs our service design and delivery so that the most effective interventions can be isolated and analyzed. Additionally, program evaluation allows us to understand and communicate our impact to a variety of stakeholders, including partners, funders, our program participants, and the general public.*

Resource allocation is just part of preparing for program evaluation. Before you start the planning process, gaining buy-in for program evaluation from staff is a critical litmus test. The next chapter outlines the importance of buy-in and how to build it in your organization.

# CHAPTER 4

# Build a Culture of Evaluation

It's critical to understand the intersection of program evaluation and organizational culture. How your staff feels and thinks about evaluation will dictate their attitudes and behaviors toward it. Are staff members doing evaluation because of a mandate from funders, or because they want the insights and learning that data can provide?

Beth Kanter and Aliza Sherman provide a clear definition of organizational culture in their book *The Happy, Healthy Nonprofit: Strategies for Impact without Burnout:* "Organizational culture is a complex tapestry made up of attitudes, values, behaviors, and artifacts of the people who work for your nonprofit."

Values and attitudes drive behaviors that make up the culture of your organization. For example, if your organization values data as a learning opportunity, you are likely to have a culture that embraces evaluation. If your organization does not value data, it is likely to become a culture of compliance (at best) with regards to evaluation.

How about your program staff? They probably present a wide range of attitudes, from enthused to resistant.

*The motivation to do program evaluation impacts how nonprofits successfully collect and use data.* Does your nonprofit feel mandated to collect data because funders require it, or are data collected for learning and continuous program improvement?

Your organization's place along the following spectrum determines the ability to build a culture of evaluation, which, in turn, affects the ability to successfully perform and use evaluation.

| A Culture of Learning vs. Compliance | |
| --- | --- |
| **Old School: Culture of Compliance** | **New School: Culture of Learning** |
| Do we Really need to do surveys with everyone? I just don't have the time for this. Don't funders know we are making a difference? Do we really have to prove it?<br><br>**BELIEFS:**<br><br>It takes too much time and money. These beliefs keep an organization in a culture of compliance, and an unwillingness to engage in evaluation work. | Will this survey help us learn more about the impact we're making? Can we use the data to change our program design, if needed? I want to be sure what we're doing is actually achieving goals.<br><br>**BELIEFS:**<br><br>Data are needed for continuous program improvement and accountability to stakeholders. These beliefs demonstrate an attitude of wanting data to learn, share, and grow. |

# From Resistance to Willingness

Here are three steps to help move an organization that's resistant to evaluation toward willingness:

1.  **Validate:** This is a brief but important step. By reflecting their concerns back to the skeptics, you are acknowledging them where they are so that a shift can begin.

2.  **Educate:** Alleviate their concerns about lack of time and money through sharing actual evaluation cost guidelines. The deeper issue is typically a lack of understanding of what evaluation is, the benefits of evaluation results, and the staff's role in the process.

3.  **Collaborate:** Making a conscious effort for program and development staff to collaborate in the planning stages is a pivotal piece in building a culture of evaluation. Common pitfalls can be avoided by employing this vital concept.

## Validate

Validation is a communication tool that's important in any conversation. When someone disagrees, rather than disagree in turn, always validate the concerns. Common phrases include:

*I hear you: Program evaluation is an expensive undertaking.*

*I understand why you feel that evaluation will take too much time.*

Reflecting their opinion, rather than refuting it, allows for people to feel heard. Validation works in a range of situations, both personal and professional.

## Educate

It's important to highlight the benefits for the individual as well as for the organization as a whole. In this way, you can shift one person's beliefs toward valuing evaluation. It's not instant—educating someone about evaluation often takes several conversations, and the building of a relationship.

A common fear is that data will show that a program is not meeting goals, even resulting in loss of jobs. Educating staff on the benefits of program evaluation can alleviate unspoken concerns and increase positivity toward evaluation. Illustrate the need for data to learn whether a program is meeting goals and, if not, what kind of improvement plan is required.

Let me tell you about an organization that had tremendous fear about negative findings and how we overcame them. I emailed them the evaluation report before our meeting. They called to tell me, "the data are wrong."

That raised my curiosity (and, honestly, my blood pressure). They had a two-year contract to coordinate a peer-learning cohort. Participants rated communications as low, with many stating they didn't understand the project, their role, and the expectations. My client insisted that they did communicate with participants, and therefore the data were wrong. They were very anxious about these results and did not want to send this report to their funder.

First, validate: "I understand your concerns about the data and that you believe you are communicating with the participants."

Second, educate: "The data are telling you to change the communication methods you're using. Let's talk about other communication methods that might work better in this situation.

Then we'll write a one-page improvement plan highlighting what we've found and how you're going to use the data to improve."

This talked them off the ledge, thankfully. The improvement plan and evaluation report were well received by the funder. In fact, a year later, the same funder increased their funding because the program staff were transparent about their "negative" findings.

A lack of time and money are also common reasons people resist program evaluation. Typically, this stems from not understanding exactly what program evaluation is and how it will benefit the organization as a whole.

Concerns about lack of money may stem from not valuing evaluation and, therefore, not wanting to spend money on it. In contrast, fears about lack of time may reveal a lack of collaborative structures organization-wide. This likely affects the organization in multiple areas, and it's likely the culture as a whole has "not enough time" for anything.

Program staff generally do the bulk of evaluation activities since they are on the front lines implementing the programs. This means ensuring that they understand how their short-term time investment in collaborating on a program evaluation system will yield long-term benefits. Some of these include taking the guesswork out of program planning, using data to make program-related decisions, and understanding how to improve the program.

As previously discussed, a common guideline is to dedicate 10 to 15 percent of a program's operating budget to evaluation activities. Ultimately, a program evaluation system will financially benefit an organization in the long run, perhaps through streamlining processes and reducing staff time on activities such as report writing or program planning which ultimately lowers staff costs. A program evaluation system may also generate reports that illustrate impact, which development staff can use to secure funds.

## Collaborate

Staff may be willing to do evaluation but unable to collaborate. This disconnect typically occurs between the development and program staff.

The level of collaboration in an organization influences evaluation capacity. If collaborative structures aren't already in place, it likely affects other areas besides program evaluation capacity.

The organization can see this as an opportunity to increase capacity in this area, using program evaluation as the vehicle to do so. Collaboration is a critical organizational factor, facilitating conversations among departments to ensure that the program evaluation plan is meaningful and realistic for everyone.

## The Spectrum of Motivation and Collaboration

Understanding where your organization falls on a spectrum of collaboration and motivation can help you see where to start shifting the culture. The following graphic offers a visual map.

Once you see where you are on the spectrum, learn how to move toward evaluation nirvana. Read on for each quadrant's characteristics, along with actions to shift toward a more balanced evaluation system.

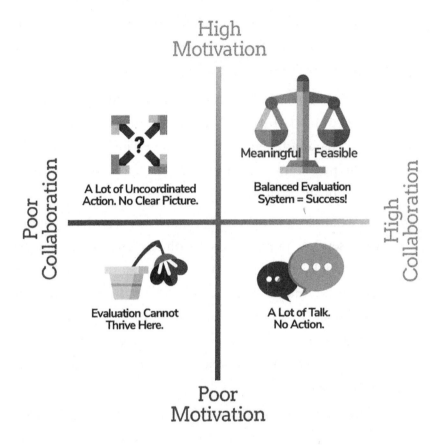

- **Low Collaboration/Low Motivation:** Evaluation cannot survive in this space. There is just too much work to do to increase collaboration and motivation before introducing evaluation planning. Always start small, expand, experience success, and then build from that progress. Choose one place to start—collaboration or motivation—and move forward from there.

- **High Motivation/Low Collaboration:** The highly motivated organization has already recognized the value of evaluation

27

work. The problem is, there are too many chefs in the kitchen, moving in different directions. Some may be doing surveys while others monitor activities, with no coordinated approach or foundation for evaluation work.

There is typically no plan for evaluation. Highly motivated data enthusiasts collect, manage, analyze, and report data independently of others. The lack of collaboration puts unneeded stress on colleagues and may result in duplicate efforts.

For example, an organization that serves youth may house three separate programs, each with its own program director and staff. Each program may then develop its own survey, measuring many of the same metrics. If they choose to collaborate, they can discover where their outcomes overlap and generate a single survey that serves the needs of all three programs. This approach is resource-efficient in terms of time and costs.

- **High Collaboration/Low Motivation:** This organization likely has lots and lots of meetings, with many interesting conversations. However, no action occurs because there is a lack of motivation for evaluation.

In this case, it is vital to have open and honest conversations about the reasons for the lack of motivation. Then shift the discussions to questions like this:

> *Do we want to know if we're making the difference we want to make? While we hear stories from our participants, how do we really know unless we have a formal structure in place?*

*Do we want to learn, grow, and change to help the people we're trying to help? Can we align what we need to learn with what funders want to know, even if it means development and program staff will need to dive into this topic together?*

**High Collaboration/High Motivation:** Congratulations, you've reached evaluation context nirvana. If you're here, you regularly collaborate on measurable outcomes, data collection activities, and program evaluation as a whole. All staff believe program evaluation is valuable and are interested in using data to learn. High fives all around!

## Example: Building a culture of evaluation (In4All)

Here's Elaine Charpentier Philippi, executive director of In4All, on how they made the shift to a culture of program evaluation:

*Building a culture of evaluation is not easy, but it is worth it! When it comes to working with your board of directors and staff, start with what you know to be true: given the choice, every one of them would want to increase outcomes for the populations your organization serves. From that posture, work to educate them in a way that is both meaningful and empathetic.*

*The following are some successful strategies I used when building a culture of evaluation in my organization:*

*Managing up. I was not the decision-maker when our cultural shift began. Taking the posture of what I knew to be true, I began to reframe the language we used to talk about impact. When we talked numbers, I mentioned outputs. When we talked about the problem and where we felt we could effect change, I mentioned outcomes. Whenever I had the chance, I would push on our reports to reflect this language. It became obvious that we were an outputs-driven organization.*

***Demonstrating.*** *One of the tools I used was a logic model. This model provided a visual roadmap that demonstrated the outcomes we should expect from a specific intervention. I built our program infrastructure from existing research defining the problem and feedback from our stakeholders on how our program could impact students. Whenever possible, back up your funding proposals with research—the data don't lie!*

*William M.K. Trochim describes the following key characteristics in his web-based textbook* Research Methods Knowledge Base. *These key characteristics/cultural identities are a handful of what you will notice when you adopt a culture of evaluation into your organization:*

***Action-oriented.*** *You find you are actively seeking solutions to problems, while not acting for action's sake but to attempt to assess the effects of your actions.*

***Truth-seeking.*** *The fear of not getting it right the first time dissipates, and you value mistakes as the learning opportunities they are. This stresses accountability and scientific credibility.*

***Forward-looking.*** *Instead of reacting to situations as they arise, you begin anticipating where evaluation feedback is most needed and can plan for implementation as part of the process.*

***Ethical and democratic.*** *You find your board of directors and staff are not interested in private ownership of and exclusive access to data and instead see it as an opportunity to contribute to best practice.*

*In a noisy world with so many of us competing to be heard, outcomes are critical. They increase validity with all stakeholders and can boost funding from individuals, foundations, and corporations. As a nonprofit leader who believes it is my responsibility to maximize our contribution to community while sticking to our core values, my commitment to evaluation is two-fold:*

1. *Outcomes bring life to my organization's unique value propositions and set us apart while contributing to change in community, AND . . .*

2. *Outcomes help us understand when our programs begin LOSING impact in real-time. This allows us to be responsive and adjust programming based on service user feedback BEFORE the funding model implodes."*

## Pitfalls to Avoid

Here are three common pitfalls to be aware of before planning. To avoid these pitfalls, be sure to collaborate across departments. One of the top reasons evaluation plans fail at implementation is a lack of buy-in.

Remember: ***Collaboration creates buy-in, which leads to successful evaluation implementation.***

### Pitfall One: Working in Isolation

This is all too common. Grant writers create new outcomes for each grant proposal, forcing them to identify what will occur as a result of a program being implemented by other people. Since it's written in isolation, the grant writer has no idea if the outcomes are actually true or not.

This common pitfall is illustrated by this story, which reflects so many others I've heard:

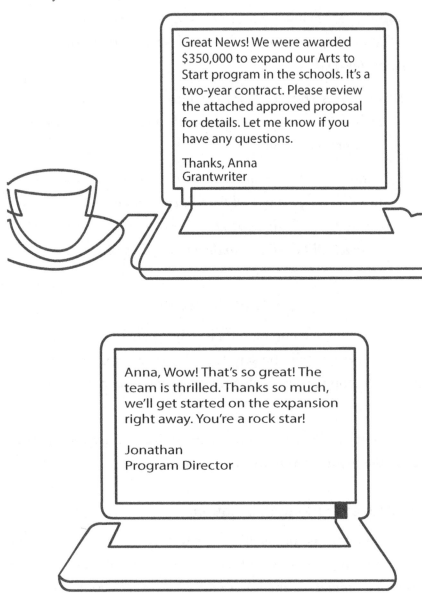

# 1 year and 50 weeks later...

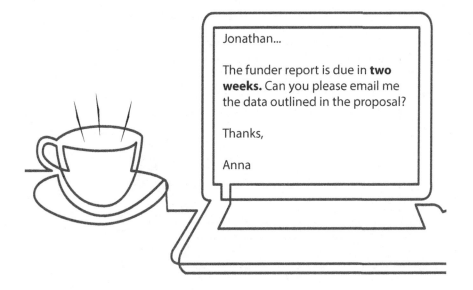

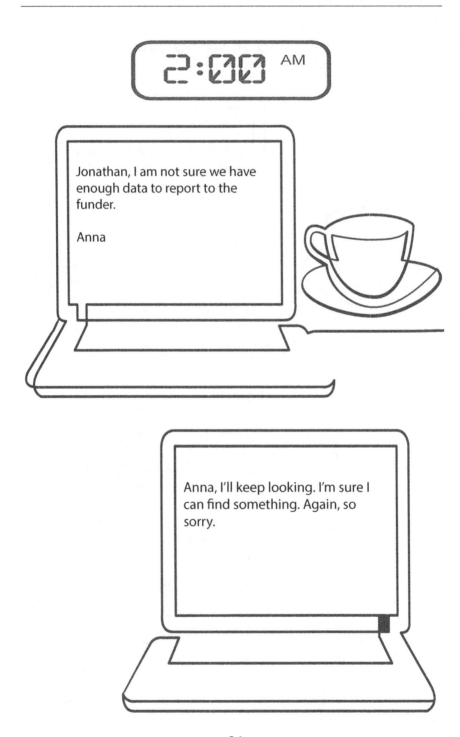

Why did this happen? Two departments didn't communicate their plan. They needed to create a shared foundation from which to draw all grant proposals. If they had worked together to create the evaluation plan, everyone would have known what data would be collected, by when, and by whom.

The solution for 2 a.m. reports is collaboration. Development and program staff need to come together and agree on outcomes to measure. Sometimes, this means compromise. What development needs to secure funds may be something program staff cannot measure, or vice versa. This requires collaboration to determine what measurable outcomes can support both development and program improvement efforts.

*It's a conversation in person. Not just emails and not in isolation. Not ever.*

Building a culture of evaluation takes time, intention, and commitment. At its core, it is about relationship building. It means understanding why people might be resistant to program evaluation and meeting them where they are.

Remember to *validate, educate,* and *collaborate* when you need to help someone shift from resistance to willingness and then to using data for learning.

## Pitfall Two: Unrealistic Ideas About Data Collection

It's easy to overestimate how much data your organization can collect. This common pitfall is caused by not enough planning in the design phase. It's often the result of a top-down decision.

For example, top management decides to do a survey, which is then created with no or little input from program staff. When the time comes for program staff to collect the data, surveys are forgotten because there wasn't enough instruction on why, how, and when to administer them.

## Example: Unrealistic Ideas about Data Collection ("Make the Grade")

Here's a fictional but reality-based example. Let's say Make the Grade is a program dedicated to helping at-risk youth improve their reading levels. There are thirty-five chapters of this organization across the United States. Each chapter implemented the program in ten to twenty-six elementary schools. Each school had a teacher who was a volunteer site coordinator. This involved identifying students to participate and coordinating tutoring schedules.

A university conducted a national evaluation of Make the Grade. The evaluation consisted of documenting the length and frequency of tutoring activities and conducting a site coordinator survey. The national evaluation team required volunteer coordinators to complete the survey composed of *three hundred questions*. The survey was obviously designed without input from chapter organizations or volunteers.

The national evaluation team pressured directors to complete the survey administration to ensure they had the data needed. Program directors tried calling volunteers and asking them to complete the survey. Can you guess the completion rate? It was only 3 percent.

Everyone was frustrated: program directors couldn't meet the national evaluation team's unrealistic requirements, and the evaluation team didn't get the data they needed for their national evaluation. This is an extreme example, where the national evaluation team overcommitted to the amount of data that could be realistically collected.

Why does this happen? A group of data enthusiasts puts a plan on paper, with no action plan of who is doing what, and without talking to those on the front lines collecting the data. Or leadership decides what will be collected in a silo, with no input from others. The plan is mandated, leading to little to no data being collected.

## Pitfall Three: No Time or Skills for Data Analysis

Sometimes data are collected, but no one has the time or skills to analyze them. The end result is five-hundred completed surveys in a filing cabinet full of data that never get used. In a typical scenario, imagine a program staff meeting where the conversation goes something like this:

"We should do a survey and see what people think!" says the program director.

"Good idea!" the staff replies. "Let's brainstorm and do that."

They create a survey and start administering it. A couple of weeks later, two staff members share their success in collecting surveys.

"Good news!" one staff member states. "I collected 150 surveys today!"

"I got two hundred! We have a lot of data," the other says, patting the stack of completed surveys.

Two months later, the stack of completed surveys has grown to five hundred. They gather in a staff meeting again.

"Great job on collecting all of these surveys!" says the program director.

The staff responds, "Thanks. So exciting."

Then the program director asks, "Who is going to analyze all of these surveys? Do any of you have experience in survey data analysis?"

Total silence.

"So," replies the program director, "no one has time or skills to analyze these surveys?"

Everyone shakes their heads. This wasn't discussed at all when they created the survey and gathered the data.

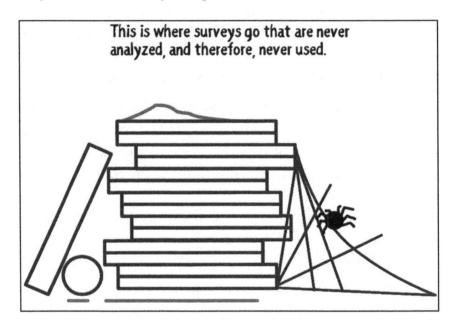

**This is where surveys go that are never analyzed, and therefore, never used.**

Why does this happen? A lack of communication and planning. In the design phase, it is critical to determine who will be doing what and by when. Before any data are collected, the plan must include who will analyze, report, communicate, and use the data. This avoids this common pitfall.

## To Avoid These Pitfalls, Slow Down

Remember: slow down, and think it through.

By slowing down, you can identify what kinds of data are both realistic and meaningful to collect.

Start by establishing a system for collecting data, such as the number of people participating. Then determine outcomes and identify a plan to evaluate them to address questions like "What impact is our program having?"

Too often, organizations jump ahead in this process by creating and administering a survey. Going slowly and thinking it through can help avoid this pitfall. Here's a helpful mantra:

*Start Small. Be Successful. Expand Your System.*

It takes collaboration to slow down and think it through. For example, in the Make the Grade scenario, the national evaluation team could have taken the time to gather input from all chapters on what is important to measure, and what is realistic for the number of survey items. This level of collaboration would have increased the likelihood of a successful national evaluation.

Thinking it through entails planning who will do what and by when. Setting up a project management timeline and evaluation activities workflow that everyone agrees is realistic helps ensure data are collected and analyzed.

It is key to assign one person to be the project manager for evaluation activities. If done internally, this is usually the program director or manager. If using an external firm, the project manager is generally the evaluator on the team. This means they oversee the process, not necessarily do all of the work.

## Questions to Consider

- Who will be the project lead for the evaluation work?
- Who is available to collect, analyze, and report data? This may be one person or separate people for those three areas.

By addressing these questions up front, the amount of data collected can be decreased or increased according to resources available to carry out evaluation activities. Doing this in the design phase avoids the common pitfalls altogether.

The next chapter addresses the importance of alignment across the entire process, setting the framework for you to get started.

# CHAPTER 5

# Align Planning with Reporting

A key element in creating a program evaluation process is alignment. We align our cars when the wheels pull to one side, and the car runs better. We align our bodies by doing yoga or going to the chiropractor, and our bodies function better.

The same is true in program evaluation. You align the difference you expect to make with what you measure. The key concept here is to *measure what matters*.

This alignment is a common thread that runs through creating the plan, collecting the data, and generating the report. When program evaluation goes off the rails, lack of alignment is often the root cause.

You have to identify the changes you want to see (*make your plan*), gather data to measure those changes (*collect your data*), and report what the data say about the expected change (*generate your reports*).

41

Too often, people rush into creating a survey without understanding what to ask. The outcomes and outputs are your anchor points, providing clear guidance for questions, survey items, intake forms, and so on.

Let's look more closely at the alignment process from planning to reporting.

## Alignment Process

1. **Make your plan**. Determine what will change (outcomes) as well as the numbers (outputs) you need to gather (i.e., participation, service hours delivered, etc.).
2. **Collect your data**. Create data collection tools such as surveys to gather data that align with outputs and outcomes.
3. **Generate your reports.** Recap outcomes and outputs alongside data that address them for a compelling summary of the results of your evaluation.

This section gives you a bird's-eye view of how to align all of these components for success. Let's get started by examining how outputs and outcomes differ when it comes to getting the data. In Part Two: Make Your Plan, we'll dive deeper into defining outcomes and outputs.

Data about outputs are generally gathered through a tracking system. This may be a simple spreadsheet or a database solution. Developing this tool requires determining what method is most resource-efficient for program staff to gather the outputs you've identified. If you're migrating to a database solution, the program evaluation plan can provide direction for the database design process.

Outcomes, on the other hand, require gathering data from program participants. Participants include people who are directly receiving services and partners involved with the implementation, as well as those who can observe changes in participants. For example, in a program that provides services directly to students, parents, or caregivers, teachers may be a good data source, since they're in a position to see changes in participants.

Tracking outputs is basic program monitoring, enabling you to state what services you provided and for how many people. The outcomes data digs deeper, illustrating how your services affected those people. In Part Two, we will delve more into creating outcomes and outputs.

Here's an example from In4All's STEM Connect™ program to illustrate the three-step alignment process, which provided consistency in communicating what they planned to do and how it ultimately went. STEM stands for Science, Technology, Engineering, and Math.

## Example: Alignment (In4All)

The In4All STEM Connect™ program partners with local STEM-focused businesses to bring real-world STEM experiences into fourth- and fifth-grade classrooms.

## Outcomes Example

1. **Make your plan.** Outcome: Students will increase their interest in STEM-related careers.
2. **Collect the data.** Pre- and post-surveys were done with fourth-grade students at a sample of the schools. The post-survey included two survey items to address this outcome. When creating the items, we realized asking about all four STEM areas would create a longer survey. It is

important to balance what will be meaningful to ask (all four areas) vs. what is realistic to ask to avoid survey fatigue (fewer areas). Therefore, In4All agreed to focus on math and science. This is a case where the outcome was altered to ensure data collection was both meaningful and realistic.

*Survey item one: Because of this program, do you feel more interested, less interested, or the same about MATH?*

*Circle one:*

   a. *More interested*
   b. *Less interested*
   c. *The same, I was already interested*
   d. *The same, I am still not interested*

*Any comments about your answer (optional):*

*Survey item two:*

*Because of this program, do you feel more interested, less interested, or the same about SCIENCE?*

   *Circle one:*

   a. *More interested*
   b. *Less interested*
   c. *The same, I was already interested.*
   d. *The same, I am still not interested.*

*Any comments about your answer (optional):*

3. **Generate the report.** Once all of the data were analyzed, the report circled back to illustrate the progress made toward the outcome. In this case, we did the same pre- and post-survey over three years. The open-ended comments came from the comments sections for the survey items, as listed above.

## Excerpt: In4All STEM Connect™ Program Student Survey Report 2016-17

### Over the last three years:

94 students with a negative or neutral interest in science in the pre-survey increased their interest in science-related careers.

159 students with a negative or neutral interest in math in the pre-survey increased their interest in math-related careers.

*Awesome, I love it.* (2017)

*When I grow up, I want to be a vet that includes math and science.* (2016)

*I would love to have a job in science when I grow up.* (2015)

*Outputs example*

In4All already had a database system in place prior to the evaluation plan. This example shows how they aligned their outputs to their database system and how those data were ultimately reported out.

1. **Make your plan.** STEM Connect™ tracks a range of outputs, including the number of businesses, volunteers from those businesses, number of schools, classes within those schools, and students.

2. **Collect your data.** The program staff gather data through Google Forms and compile them in Excel.

   • Volunteers: They collect volunteer lists from partner companies for matching—the total comes from that list.

- Teachers: Each school provides a class list on their school profile form, indicating the number of classrooms they are doing programming in.
- Students: Schools report numbers of students in each class listed on the profile form.
- Numbers of schools and businesses: This is drawn from the number of Memorandums of Understanding (MOUs) from schools and businesses.

3. **Generate your reports.** The 2016 Stakeholder Report highlighted the following outputs:

167 volunteers

115 classrooms

2,957 students

This was presented alongside the outcome data. The combination of illustrating who participated alongside program impacts provides a comprehensive picture of the degree to which STEM Connect™ is *creating a pathway to a STEM career.*

This extensive example illustrates how to define outputs and outcomes to be in total alignment. It required thoughtful collaboration to create outcomes and outputs as defined in the evaluation plan. These anchor points served as a springboard for creating data collection tools to gather data aligned to the outputs and outcomes.

The student pre- and post-surveys, teacher surveys, and business partner surveys all focused on gathering data aligned to those outcomes. Outputs tracked activities, providing them with a holistic picture of what went well, what needed improvement, and the overall impact. The data then funneled into a compelling report, which also aligned to the original outcomes and outputs— empowering them to share with confidence the difference STEM Connect™ makes, as well as opportunities to improve.

Now your resources are in place to move forward. You understand how to build a culture of evaluation to ensure the evaluation process is implemented with fidelity, and data are used to improve programs and show impact. You understand the role alignment plays throughout the program evaluation process. It's time to move on to Part Two: Make Your Plan.

## Part Two

# MAKE YOUR PLAN

Evaluation planning ensures that realistic outcomes are defined together. The outcomes are relevant both to program and development staff. This planning process positions your organization to use data to make decisions, taking the guesswork out of how to plan your programs as well as what data to report to funders.

Jean Hansen, Vice President of School Partnerships and Youth Outreach for Special Olympics Oregon, has this to share:

> One of the best processes was in the beginning of the program evaluation work, going through creating measurable outcomes and how they align with program activities. That got us focused on what it was we wanted to accomplish. We wrote the grant, really didn't have a plan for program implementation. That process helped to organize things.

The program staff typically manages the evaluation process. While other departments, such as development, marketing, communications, and others, will use the data, program staff are usually the ones to collect it. Therefore, the program director typically takes the reins of the planning process, ensuring the data collection activities are realistic as well as meaningful.

If you have multiple programs, you can start with one program and then scale the planning process to other departments. If you are starting with one program, choose the one with the most direct and straightforward outcomes and a program director who is already on board with the evaluation process. Alternatively, all program directors may form a workgroup to develop an organization-wide evaluation system collaboratively.

You'll need to collaborate on tackling the following questions:

- What exactly does your program do?
- What change is expected as a result?
- How will you measure that change?

Part Two provides details on how to answer these questions through engaging in discovery, creating a logic or impact model, and identifying methods to measure what matters.

# CHAPTER 6

# Engage in Discovery

For the program evaluation plan, you need critical thinking to ensure you clearly define what your program does. This includes answering two key questions:

- What does your program do?
- What difference do you expect it to make?

You may already have a program description on your website and in your marketing materials and grant proposals.

Some organizations have a communication gap around their programs. The discovery process closes that gap, so when you move onto defining program evaluation elements, you're already clear on what exactly the program does.

Discovery may be an instance where an outside facilitator can help you clarify and align your understanding as an organization.

## Example: Discovery (Candlelighters)

Candlelighters for Children with Cancer puts on a yearly family camp. Before discovery, this was their program description:

*For more than eighteen years, Candlelighters has held a Family Camp program at Camp Harlow in Eugene, Oregon, over Labor Day weekend. This three-day weekend camp brings together families from throughout Oregon and Southwest Washington who are unified by the shared experience of pediatric cancer.*

The discovery process included two key activities:

- A document analysis of all written materials regarding the camp
- A brief open-ended survey with staff and board members

These sources revealed a gap between the camp activities and what staff reported as the impact of Family Camp on the participants. For instance, camp activities included swimming, crafts, and family movie night. Program impact described by staff included statements like these: *Lessen isolation and depression*, *Create a source of strength*, and *Gain support for entire families.*

How do swimming, campfires, and arts and crafts result in the significant impact identified by the key stakeholders? Short answer: they don't. Something was missing.

Identifying this gap led to the development of a new program framework, which effectively linked activities and impact. They realized it isn't traditional camp activities that are important in Family Camp—it's the conversations and interactions that happen during those activities. Active participation in the Family Camp activities contributed to each individual's social, emotional, and learning needs.

The input survey results revealed new ways the camp was supporting families, including facilitating social connections, providing emotional support, and sharing tips for navigating the medical and financial systems. This was nowhere in their written materials, though it was clearly an essential part of their impact.

They closed the activity-to-impact gap by inserting the following outcome categories, which further defined program impacts:

- **Social:** Activities that promote interaction and having fun.
- **Emotional:** Activities that help create a coping framework for this journey.
- **Knowledge:** Activities that promote sharing lessons and learning from each other.

Adding these categories to describe the impact on participants enabled them to measure the degree to which desired outcomes were being fulfilled. Showing how camp activities can lead to deep impact, they improved their ability to communicate about the Family Camp program. After the program evaluation plan was completed, they used the impact model to describe their program in a different and more targeted way.

Your discovery process may find that your program description needs no changes at all, or it may need to be entirely revised. To get started, complete these two key activities:

1. **Document analysis.** Review all written materials, such as grant proposals, web content, and marketing materials. Grant proposals are a great source for persuasively articulating what the program does.
   - *Do they all say the same things about the program? If not, how are they different? If so, what are the messages about program goals, activities, and outcomes/impact?*

Use these responses to generate a new program description that synthesizes all written materials.

2. **Staff/board input.** Survey staff and board to understand their opinions regarding the program description. Ask the following questions via email or use an online survey program if that's easier to view all responses by question:
   - *What is the overall goal of this program?*
   - *What are the key activities of our program?*
   - *What impact do you believe it makes on participants?*

   Review the survey results, considering the following:
   - *Do the staff/board members agree or disagree with each other in these three areas? How can this be resolved?*
   - *Did new concepts emerge that are not in the written materials?*

If changes are needed to your program description, follow these steps:

1. **Rewrite the program goal, activities, and intended impact** based on the document analysis and input survey results.
2. **Create a new description** with staff and board. (An outside facilitator may be helpful here.)
3. **Finalize new program goals, activities, and impact** with buy-in from staff and board.

The process brings these questions into focus:
- *What are the program activities?*
- *Are these activities described the same way across all written materials? If not, how can they be aligned?*
- *Is it plausible for these activities to make a difference in participants' lives?*
- *Are there goals, outcomes, or other descriptions of expected change?*

## Example: Discovery (Portland Homeless Family Services)

PHFS operated two shelters: Goose Hollow at night and Thirteen Salmon Family Center in the daytime. Shelters were operated by staff and volunteers, serving eight homeless families at a time.

Their ultimate goal was to get families housed. Marketing materials and grant proposals highlighted program activities such as case management and life skills classes to achieve this goal. In the staff/board input survey, many stated the relationships formed between staff and families provided the trust and support needed for families to become housed. This sentiment was not reflected in their written materials.

During discovery, it was observed that staff provided a tremendous amount of emotional support, case management, and logistical support. They helped families to research housing options and apply for housing, as well as to pursue educational opportunities, which increased the parents' chance of remaining employed and therefore housed.

The question arose: where was the explicit description of how these emotional, cognitive, and physical needs were being met for these families? A new program framework emerged, improving the alignment between program activities and expected impact. Program activities were categorized as shown on the following chart.

## PHFS Shelter Program Description Post-discovery

| Area of Need | Shelter Program Activity |
|---|---|
| Physical | Facilities to ensure basic needs are met: food, shelter, and clothing |
| | Childcare for preschool children and after-school activities for school-age children |
| | Each family gets its own room |
| | Showers, laundry, and toiletries available |
| Emotional | Emotional support from volunteers and staff |
| | Community dinner served by volunteers on a nightly basis |
| | Create relationships with families through a support network of volunteers and staff |
| | Weekly meetings with a housing specialist |
| Cognitive/educational | Access to computers, internet, and printers |
| | Life skills program three times a week with classes such as budgeting, parenting, and healthy relationships |
| | Rent Well program to understand tenant rights |

By reviewing all of the documents and gathering staff/board input, a new description of your program and its impact may emerge. This is the description you want to use moving forward with the evaluation planning process. For consistency, use this new description in all future marketing, communications, and development materials.

Next, you need to clearly articulate what change you expect your program to make in the form of change or outcome statements.

# CHAPTER 7

# Define Measurable Outcomes

Several decades ago, outputs were acceptable by funders as evaluation results. But outputs provide only the numbers of people participating and/or service hours delivered; they do not provide information on actual change that occurred as a result of program activities.

Sheri Chaney Jones, president of Measurement Resources, captures this in her blog post, "Outputs v. Outcomes Matters" (February 2, 2014): "McDonalds sells 33 billion burgers per day. Five Guys sells 350,000 burgers per day. Can you tell by just sales who makes the better burger?"

No. Sales numbers just tell you who sells more. McDonald's may sell more because theirs is cheaper, they have more locations, etc. They have nothing to do with which one is better.

The same is true for outputs. Just from the numbers, you can't tell if a program is making a difference because five hundred people participated or 250 service hours were delivered. You still need to track this information to report participation, but it doesn't tell you anything about change.

An outcome statement is a change statement. What changes do you expect as a result of program activities?

Outcome statements drive the design of data collection tools. If you expect that students will increase their interest in STEM-related careers, then that is what you need to measure.

Development staff members can use outcome statements in grant proposals and other development activities. Program staff must buy into the outcome statements, believing both that they are achievable and realistic to measure. As discussed in Chapter 4, Build a Culture of Evaluation, collaboratively creating outcomes avoids 2 a.m. report writing.

*By creating outcomes together, development staff know what to promise in their grant proposals, and program staff know what data to collect.*

Measurable outcomes are the cornerstone of your evaluation plan. I developed the process and formula described in the next few pages to facilitate collaboration between development and program staff. I've taught it hundreds of times in workshops and have seen it work to demystify measurable outcomes.

## Formula for Measurable Outcomes

1. **Begin with an action.** Terms to use include *increase, improve, decrease, gain, create, expand, reduce,* and *maintain.*
2. **State what will change:** knowledge, behavior, skills, or attitudes. Here are some questions to consider and examples:

    **Knowledge**: What do you expect participants to understand or know more about?

*Improve understanding of lease compliance rules*

*Increase students' understanding of STEM-related careers*

**Behavior:** How did behavior change as a result of program activities?

*A decrease in unhealthy food choices or an increase in healthy food choices*

**Skills:** What measurable skills changed as a result of program activities?

*Improve participants' budgeting skills*

**Attitude:** How did participants' attitudes change as a result of program activities?

*Improve attitudes toward math*

3. **Note which group is intended to benefit from the outcome,** such as seniors, youth, community members, etc.

Once statements emerge, discuss each one and how they truly relate to the program. Ask these questions:

- *Is this outcome in alignment with the program activities?*
- *Will the outcome help staff with program improvement?*
- *Will the outcome help staff with development efforts?*
- *Is it measurable?*

The questions about helping staff are critical. Sometimes what program managers can and want to measure is different from what development staff needs to secure funds.

How to resolve that? Compromise. Development staff may want specific data to secure funds, but program staff either can't collect those data or do not believe the outcome or output is relevant to the program.

For example, imagine an organization that helps immigrants understand how to become a United States citizen. Program staff help participants understand the process but do not actually help them complete the process from beginning to end. The grant writer wants to measure the following output:

## Increase the Number of Immigrants Who Secure Citizenship

But program staff doesn't have a system in place to track the people they serve after participation has ended. And such a system would be hard to implement since it would require tracking people once they have left their program to see if they did apply the knowledge they acquired to become U.S. citizens.

In cases like this, it's important to think beyond what you can't do and instead focus on what you want and can do. One possible solution: change from an output to a measurable outcome.

## Improve Immigrants' Understanding of How to Secure Citizenship

Program staff could administer a post-survey to participants, asking questions to demonstrate knowledge of how to secure citizenship. While this doesn't provide the number of participants who actually achieved citizenship as a result of their participation, it does show how their knowledge did or did not change.

Whether an outcome is measurable depends on what you are trying to understand. First, brainstorm a list of outcomes, probably more than will make it to the final list. Then gain agreement on what the outcomes will be.

It is perfectly fine if you get into designing your surveys or interview question guides and discover that an outcome needs refinement to be measurable, or perhaps it isn't measurable after all. In those cases, it's helpful to revisit what change you're trying to achieve and how to measure it.

Finalizing measurable outcomes may be an opportunity to bring in an outside expert. The expert can review your outcomes and determine whether existing data collection tools address your outcomes or you need to create new ones. Engaging an expert to finalize data collection tools may be a better use of resources, depending upon the complexity of your outcomes and your staff's expertise in this area.

Typically, a program will have two to seven measurable outcomes. As a part of the logic or impact model, having too many outcomes would spill onto additional pages, while too few don't provide enough information about changes to expect. Too many outcomes may also lead to trying to measure more than is feasible. Prioritizing outcomes focuses your data collection efforts, ensuring what you are measuring is both meaningful and realistic.

Now that you have answered what your program does and what change you expect it to make, you are ready to take on the next step in the evaluation planning process: creating your logic or impact model.

# CHAPTER 8

# Create Your Logic or Impact Model

A *logic model* is a linear one-page document that defines a program's goals, activities, outputs, inputs, outcomes, and impact. Logic models serve an important role as a visual summary of the program. This visualization is essential to get everyone literally on the same page. Ideally, it's created at the start of program design.

The go-to resource for creating a logic model is W.K Kellogg Foundation's *Logic Model Development Guide* (2004), which defines a logic model as follows:

> *The program logic model is defined as a picture of how your organization does its work—the theory and assumptions underlying the program. A logic model links outcomes (both short- and long-term) with program activities/processes and the theoretical assumptions/principles of the program.*

Working with clients, I've learned that some people just don't like logic models. When they hear the term, a nervous quiver runs down their spine, perhaps post-traumatic stress from a bad experience. These clients want a visual summary, but they don't like the logic model's cookie-cutter approach.

In response, I developed the *impact model*. It still answers the two core questions: what does your program do, and what change is expected as a result? But it departs from the traditional linear format to include whatever information and format your organization will use. The impact model reflects your organization's culture, right down to brand colors, making it usable in development, marketing, and communications efforts.

Both models provide direction and clarity for program evaluation, along with an insight into what methodology and measurements to use and a framework for discussing program evaluation elements with staff.

You be the judge of what is truly best. If you have to create a logic model to satisfy a funder, do that. If you prefer a customized visual summary, do an impact model instead.

At the end of the day, you want a visual summary that depicts what your program does and what change is expected as a result.

Read through the rest of this chapter to see which model best represents your program. Either way, you'll want to start by defining the elements of the logic model, since you'll need them for both models.

## The Logic Model

A logic model provides a one-page summary of what a program does and what change is expected as a result. Often, federal grants require a logic model. It includes these elements, arranged in a linear format:

- **Goals:** What do we hope to change at a broad level?
- **Inputs:** What resources will we invest as part of our program?
- **Activities:** What events, action steps, or activities will happen as part of our program?
- **Outputs:** What does our program produce? (i.e., attendees, materials distributed, membership renewed, intake forms, events, etc.)
- **Outcomes:** What actually changed for our participants?

Alignment is a cornerstone of any logic or impact model. Can you see the alignment across all five areas in the example below?

## Example: Logic Model ("Youth Tutoring Program")

Here's an example of a fictitious youth tutoring program. We'll use examples from this program throughout this section.

| Goal | Inputs | Activities | Outputs | Outcomes |
|------|--------|-----------|---------|----------|
| To improve the academic achievement of students so they can achieve their full academic potential | Three tutors<br><br>Space for tutoring sessions<br><br>Tutoring plan created in collaboration with schools | Number of students tutored<br><br>Number of tutoring sessions<br><br>Number of participating schools | Number of students tutored<br><br>Number of tutoring sessions<br><br>Number of participating schools | Improve student academic performance.<br><br>Increase school attendance |

The common themes are students and academic success. The five components flow from the big picture—the goal—to the measurable change expected to occur—the outcomes. The overall flow shows what is going into the program (inputs and activities), followed by what the results of the program will be (outputs and outcomes).

## The importance of alignment

When you create your logic model, it is crucial to ensure alignment across all of the components. At a minimum, development and program staff should agree upon these core components to avoid 2 a.m. report writing.

If you're a grant writer, you may be tempted to write the logic model on your own to be time-efficient. I caution you to avoid this, as it will likely cost more time down the road when program staff do not have the data you determined they should collect.

Instead, determine together what measurable outputs and outcomes are realistic and meaningful to collect for both program improvement purposes as well as to secure funds. This may be time-intensive on the front end, but it will make everyone's lives much easier when the time comes to report on outputs and outcomes.

## Logic model elements

The following breaks down how to define each of the logic model components. As you do your own, keep in mind all of these components should look related:

### Goal

Your goal is a broad statement of what you hope to change. It is focused on the broad strokes; it is not specific or measurable. It should also align with your mission statement.

Take the goal statement from the example above: *to improve the academic achievement of students so they can achieve their full academic potential.* "Improve academic achievement" and "full academic potential" address in general ways how the program is intended to help students. It is clear from this statement they are providing services to students, so there's an overall understanding of what the program does.

Examples for other program types include:

- *To help teaching artists connect with each other and themselves to deepen their teaching practice*
- *To provide resources, relationships, and advocacy to help end homelessness*

## Inputs

Inputs refer to the resources for a program to operate, including people, space, equipment, funds, and anything or anyone else that's needed. Inputs are what you *put into* a program so it can run.

If you need a traditional logic model to fulfill funder requirements, plan on including inputs. Otherwise, you may not need this element to describe what your program does and what difference it makes.

### Example: Inputs ("Youth Tutoring Program")

The Youth Tutoring Program logic model example includes three inputs: *three tutors, space for tutoring sessions,* and *tutoring plan created in collaboration with schools.* Other input examples:

- *Staff (FTE) to run the program*
- *Partnerships*
- *Materials (handouts, curriculum)*
- *Equipment (computers, phones)*

## Activities

Activities are the essential actions that make your program go. They're what you talk about when someone asks what your program does. In the previous chapter, you already did a deep dive into program activities.

*Example: Activities ("Youth Tutoring Program")*

For the Youth Tutoring program, activities *provide academic instruction at least twice a week* and *provide ongoing guidance to encourage school attendance and increase hours spent on schoolwork.* These two activities are clearly aligned to the goal and inputs, illustrating the specifics of how the program is carried out. Here are more sample activities:

- *Provide math and science activities in fourth- and fifth-grade classrooms*
- *Deliver food boxes to homeless shelters*
- *Provide sight and hearing screening for people without access to quality health care for hearing and vision*

## Outputs

Outputs are the measurable evidence that your program is operating. They show the level of participation, but not necessarily what kind of difference the program is making.

## Example: Outputs ("Youth Tutoring Program")

In the Youth Tutoring Program logic model example, outputs are the numbers of students, tutoring sessions delivered, and participating schools. Other example outputs include:

- *Number of food boxes delivered*
- *Number of patients treated*
- *Number of homeless families housed*

## Outcomes

Outcomes measure changes as a result of the program in terms of knowledge, skills, attitudes and/or behavior. Outcomes are a key ingredient in the program evaluation plan.

## Example: Outcomes ("Youth Tutoring Program")

In the Youth Tutoring Program logic model example, as a result of participating in the program, student behavior toward attendance is expected to change. They also expect student academic skills to improve as a result of the program, resulting in higher grades. Some other sample outcome statements include:

- *To increase students interest in STEM-related careers*
- *To improve housing stability*
- *To improve health conditions for low-income residents*

## Worksheet: Logic model

Use the following worksheet with staff members to define key logic model components. If you prefer, you can draft ideas to give staff something to discuss, rather than starting with a blank page.

| | Goal |
|---|---|
| | Inputs |
| | Activities |
| | Outputs |
| | Outcomes |

# The Impact Model

For some organizations, an impact model may be a better fit than a logic model. This is a model I created that blends logic model components with visualization techniques and can be used for evaluation as well as development, marketing, and communications.

It still addresses the questions of what your program does and what change is expected as a result, but it includes other relevant information for your program. You can add information to your impact model so that it clearly communicates your intended program impact. Elements include:

- **Structure**: This provides an overview of what your program does, program goal, who it is for, and who is involved with delivering it. It typically takes about the top third or so of the letter-size page.
- **Activities:** Just as in the logic model, the program activities define what exactly you are providing to participants.
- **Outcomes:** Also, as in the logic model, this includes what measurable change is expected to occur as a result of program activities.

These three sections are at the core of the impact model. From there, it's customized to reflect each program's unique offerings. Other sections include measurements, outputs, inputs, assumptions, and other relevant information to help clearly communicate what your program does and what change is expected as a result.

For example, the Candlelighters Family Camp included that their program removes both financial and geographic barriers, two key program aspects. They decided their model didn't need inputs or outputs to communicate their intended impact.

In Dr. Stephanie Evergreen's book, *Presenting Data Effectively*, she details the pictorial superiority effect. Because we take in so much information with our eyes, using visualization to communicate is a powerful method. The impact model may utilize the organization's brand colors, infographics, and other visual elements.

Every program is unique. Customize your impact model to reflect your program as well as your organization as a whole. It still needs to answer the key questions:

- What does your program do?
- What change is expected as a result?

Start with a design concept, outlining sections and points to include. Be sure that your program model, activities, and outcomes are defined and agreed upon by program and development staff, at least, before moving into the graphic design phase.

## Impact Model Examples

Start with high-level information to set the foundation of what your program is all about, including who is delivering the program and the overall goal.

You may include just the goal, activities and outcomes in your impact model, or expand it to include how you will measure progress toward outcomes, how many people you serve, and other items unique to your program. Remember, the key is to visually summarize what your program does and what impact you intend it to make.

For full-page, full-color examples of impact models, visit the companion website 🖥: www.evaluationintoaction.com/getyourdata.

## Example: Impact Model Design Concept (Candlelighters)

*Program description:* Family camp is a three-day weekend for families experiencing pediatric cancer.

*People involved with delivering the program:*

- *Four Candlelighters staff*
- *Two healthcare providers*
- *Eight to ten volunteers*

*Program goal:* Create a community support system that will improve the overall quality of life for families experiencing pediatric cancer.

Sometimes important aspects of your program do not fall within the categories of goals, activities, and outcomes. This was the case for Candlelighters. An important aspect of their program was described in their model as follows:

*Remove geographic barriers:* Families experiencing pediatric cancer are from Oregon and SW Washington. The Family Camp removes these geographic barriers, creating a safe space for them to connect.

*Remove financial barriers:* Camp is provided free of charge, which decreases financial barriers to participation.

Next, include activities, which can be pulled from your program description or the activities you defined in the previous section. Since you have just one page, be very clear about what you're going to communicate. Here's what Candlelighters did for the Family Camp program activities:

### Candlelighters Program Activities

*Create opportunities to connect*

*Traditional camp activities facilitate conversations and connections.*

*Art Shack/Art Therapy, Bumper Boats/Go-Carts, Campfire, Educational Workshops, Family Photos, Haircuts/Makeovers, Horse Trail Rides, Magic Show, Community Meals, Parent Meditation Workshop, Parent Social Hour, Rock Wall, Teen-focused Activities, Yoga*

*Camp activities range from contemplative (meditation workshops) to interactive (parent social hour). All activities seek to create a community support system.*

In the last section, include your outcomes. In some cases, you may need a transition statement to help link activities to outcomes. Exactly why will these activities result in these outcomes?

Candlelighters required a bridge between activities and outcomes, illustrating how the *conversations and connections* that occurred during family camp activities helped fulfill their outcomes.

### Candlelighters Outcomes

The **conversations and connections** that occur **during** these *traditional camp activities impact participants in the following ways:*

| Outcomes | | |
|---|---|---|
| Expand social connections with other families experiencing pediatric cancer | Establish an emotional coping framework | Increase knowledge about how to navigate the medical process and financial resources |

## Example: Impact Model Design Concept (NHA)

To understand how much this can vary program to program, let's look at this example from Northwest Housing Alternatives (NHA). The NHA resident services program goal is the overarching concept under which the program activities, outcomes, and measurement methods fall. The first part of their impact model includes the following information:

### Program structure

| |
|---|
| Program goal: To connect residents to services that promote housing stability |
| Six resident services coordinators (RSC) |
| Liaison between residents and fulfilling resident needs |
| Assumption: Fulfilling resident needs will increase the likelihood that they will remain housed |
| Available to: 2600 residents across 31 properties |

The Program Structure section summarizes what your program does. Generally, it's a service provider overview of your program. It leads into the program activities.

NHA's discovery process revealed two distinct ways activities are delivered: directly by resident services coordinators and coordinated by RSCs with a service partner. It was important to define these as two separate components so that NHA staff could measure how well each type of activity promoted housing stability.

## Program activities

| Services are delivered by Resident Service Coordinators (RSCs) directly or coordinated with a service partner. Residents are seniors, families, or individuals with mental or physical disabilities. | |
| --- | --- |
| **Direct services**<br>**Six RSCs** | **Coordinated services**<br>**69 Service Partners** |
| • Assist with making phone calls<br>• Notice intervention/lease compliance<br>• Eviction prevention<br>• Conflict mediation with other tenants and/or property managers<br>• Individual Development Account (IDA) program<br>• Social events | • On-site programs: Adult education, health and wellness, financial education, mentoring, and youth engagement<br>• Assistance: Legal, employment, rent, utility, childcare resources, tax, emergency food boxes, and health/wellness |

In this example, program activities were collaboratively defined by staff members and aligned to activities listed above, with the intention for outcomes to occur as a result of activities.

| Expected outcomes of services delivered |
| --- |
| **Create** a sense of community within the property |
| **Improve** sense of feeling supported |
| **Decrease** negative behavior that can result in conflicts, eviction rate |
| **Increase** knowledge in identified areas of need and interest, self-sufficiency, understanding of notice prevention and lease compliance |

It made sense to add a section to the impact model describing their methods of measuring progress toward all outcomes.

| Measurement methods |
| --- |
| Intake upon service request: Track services delivered and eviction rates |
| Housing Stability Scale Ratings on a regular basis |
| Annual surveys for service partners, property managers, and residents |

## Questions to Consider

- What is your program's goal?
- Who is involved with delivering the model?
- How many people are in each of those categories?
- How many people is it delivered to?
- Any program aspects to include that are a part of your delivery model?
- Are there any assumption statements you need to include?
- What are your core activities?
- What are your measurable outcomes?
- How will you measure progress toward those outcomes?

At this point, you have the ingredients to create the first part of your plan. Before moving to the next chapter, answer these questions:

- Are you going to create a logic model, impact model, or both?
- If a logic model, did you complete the logic model worksheet collaboratively defining all components?

- If an impact model, how will you create it? What components do you need to add besides program goal, activities, and outcomes? Do you have an internal graphic designer or someone who has these skills on staff, or will you need to retain an outside expert?

Once the model is complete, share it with all staff and board members for final comments. This should be done in person, not via email, to encourage staff and board to identify with the model. In some cases, you can post a physical copy of the model in a central location, like a meeting room.

Now you're ready to move to the next chapter on methodology, where you'll determine how best to collect data to measure progress toward outcomes.

CHAPTER 9

# Determine Your Methodology

Methodology is the way you plan to collect data on outputs and outcomes.

While outputs and outcomes tell you what to measure, the methods in your methodology provide the actual data. Good alignment between what you intend to measure (outputs and outcomes) and how you measure it (methodology) ensures a clear and consistent focus on what you will report out.

Here is an excerpt from *Evaluation Mini-Guide #2: Measurement Methods and Tools,* by Kelly Jarvis and Chari Smith:

*Evaluation research commonly employs a "mixed-method" approach, which includes collecting both qualitative and quantitative data. This method provides a balance of gathering the stories (qualitative) and the numbers (quantitative) jointly used to monitor the program's progress, guide its improvement, and understand its impact.*

*There are several different types of measurement methods, including:*

- *Surveys, which can be administered in person (paper and pencil), online, or by mail; can vary in length; and are generally cost-effective.*

---

If you're going to do program evaluation without a professional evaluator, start with surveys. This book can walk you through creating a basic survey using measurable outcomes as a guide.

Surveys are less expensive than other methodologies, internal staff can administer them without risking participant bias, and they can be modified for use with multiple groups. They also offer the opportunity to gather both qualitative data through open-ended questions and quantitative data through closed-ended questions.

---

The *Evaluation Mini-Guide* outlines other methods to consider using if you want to use a third-party professional trained in these approaches.

- **Focus groups** *are conducted in person with five to ten attendees. They typically follow a semi-structured format, whereby a list of discussion questions/topics structures the conversation, but participants can bring up additional topics.*
- **Interviews** *are conducted with one participant at a time and can be done in person or over the phone (including video). They can follow either semi-structured or structured formats.*
- **Observations** *can be conducted with a variety of events and occur when the evaluator observes an event, either in person or*

*via video, and rates specific elements of the event. For example, evaluators can observe program delivery (e.g., curriculum sessions and presentations), and staff can observe participants' presentations or performances. Collecting observational data requires that a protocol and a rating scheme be developed beforehand and that observers are trained on both.*

- **Document review** *can apply to various types of materials, including participant applications, reports, or portfolios. Similar to collecting observational data, evaluators must develop a review protocol and rating scheme beforehand and train all reviewers to ensure consistency. Then, materials are reviewed and rated for the specific, relevant elements.*

It is wise to use an outside expert for methods like interviews and focus groups. Third-party evaluators are objective, so they can conduct these methods in an unbiased manner. Participants are more likely to honestly share their thoughts with someone outside of the program. Someone from your staff conducting individual phone interviews would have a greater stake in wanting to hear positive feedback about the program. A trained research or evaluation professional brings an objective lens to these methodologies, ensuring you're getting truthful data—positive or negative.

Quantitative data lends itself to measuring change over time and progress toward goals, while qualitative data can provide insight into program functioning and participant perceptions. Qualitative data gathers stories, which make for compelling communications and fundraising copy. Remember to use the names of people and organizations only if you have written permission to do so.

## Methodology Overview

This book divides methodology into two sections, addressing these questions:

1. **Process evaluation: How effectively are we implementing our programs?**

    This is an internal exploration of how well programs are being implemented. Are there opportunities to create a system that will streamline processes to gather data we're already gathering? To omit or add activities to help staff better organize their time? Essentially, this is an organizational development tool. The link between organizational development and program evaluation is clear in this capacity.

2. **Outcome evaluation: What impact is our program having on our participants?**

    Most funders are most interested in this piece. This also refers to the outcomes defined in your logic model, illustrating how your program is making a difference. And, if data show it is not making the difference you thought, how will you change your program plan accordingly?

This book uses these methods to gather data that align with both outcomes and outputs:

- **Surveys**. This is a flexible and cost-effective approach, offering many ways to gather data to measure both implementation and impact.
- **Program data**. This covers a wide range, from the number of participants for funder reporting to activities data to improve implementation. Managing your program data starts with identifying what you need to collect, from whom, and how.

## Data Sources

Both surveys and program data require understanding where and from whom to collect data. These are your data sources. They can include program participants, staff, people involved with participants, and so on. For example, a program for students may gather data from students, teachers, program staff, and principals.

The Methodology section of your evaluation plan outlines who will participate in evaluation activities (data sources) and how you will gather the data (for example, surveys). Too often, program participants are the only data source, which misses the opportunity to strengthen your story by presenting multiple points of view on the same outcome. The following illustration depicts a single data source.

### Single data source

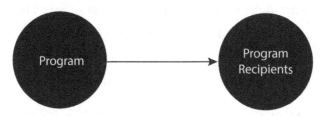

What you want to identify are all data sources—the program recipients, program staff delivering the program, and observers of the program recipients. All of these groups have valuable insights as to what is working, not working, and overall impact. The illustration below shows multiple data sources.

## Multiple data sources

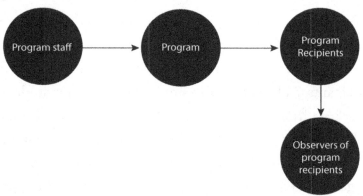

For example, let's look at the Youth Tutoring program previously discussed. It has students as participants. Gathering data from teachers, parents, and others who observed the program's impact on the student would strengthen the story by increasing the number of data points on the same outcomes and outputs. The tutors who are delivering the program are another valuable data source. The illustration below shows the relationship between these groups, and how multiple data sources can provide a more in-depth picture of how this program is working.

## Example Multiple data sources: Youth Tutoring Program

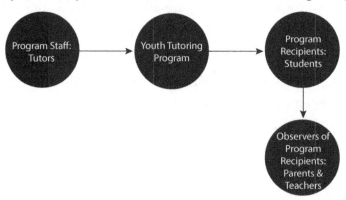

Let's look at another example. The NW Housing Alternatives used multiple data sources to measure progress toward their goals and outcomes for the Resident Services program. Surveys were administered to residents, property managers, and service providers. Questions revolved around the same goal and outcomes. The resident service coordinators (program staff) completed a housing stability rating for each resident to measure promoting housing stability. As the illustration below shows, program staff, recipients, and observers were all data sources.

## Example multiple data sources: Northwest Housing Alternatives

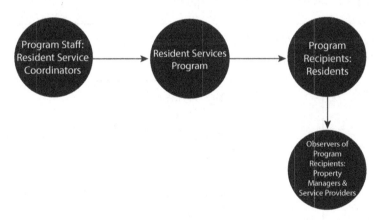

The report included data on each outcome from three different sources—residents, property managers, and service providers—rather than just residents. This strengthened their story and included feedback from groups involved with different aspects of their program. The housing stability ratings completed by program staff added a fourth data source. These ratings provided additional insight into how residents were doing and which program activities would benefit them most.

## Questions to Consider

- Who participates in your program? (e.g., low income residents, youth, seniors, etc.)
- How many staff deliver the program?
- Do you have any partners you coordinate with to deliver the program? If yes, who?
- Are there any groups that observe the impact the program may have on the participants? If so, who are they?

Using the worksheet below, fill in the groups that comprise your data sources. You will use this later when developing the surveys.

## Multiple Data Sources Template

| Program staff | Program delivered | Data source #1: |
|---|---|---|
| | | Data source #2: |
| | | Data source #3: |
| | | Data source #4: |

# CHAPTER 10

# Develop the Timeline and Workflow

Project management is a critical component of your evaluation plan. It can be easily overlooked, leaving staff scrambling to gather data in a timely fashion. We're all busy, and it's just too easy for survey administration to fall through the cracks.

A well-thought-out timeline and workflow help ensure that your program evaluation plan is actually implemented and used.

## Questions to Consider

- **Who will manage the project?** Assign a compulsively organized person as the project manager for the evaluation plan. This person does not necessarily do all the data collection, analysis, and reporting. Rather, the planning phase involves figuring out who will do all of that and by when. The project manager oversees that everyone is doing their parts to implement the plan.

- **Who will collect the data?** Typically, this falls to program staff since they are on the front lines of implementing the program. If you decide to employ an outside expert, be sure to work with them to determine who is responsible for doing what.

  For example, if you've hired an expert to do phone interviews with participants, you may be responsible for communicating expectations, setting the schedule, and other logistics. This will streamline the process for when the expert receives the phone schedule and conducts the interviews.

- **When will the data be collected?** Review your program implementation timeline and determine when is the most realistic and meaningful period to gather the data.

  This is unique to each organization. If your program has a beginning and an end, then a logical time to administer a survey would be mid-program and at the end. If your program is continuous, typically gathering data on an annual basis will suffice.

- **Who will analyze and report the data?** This may be more than one person. Thinking through who has the time, capacity, and expertise will allow you to avoid the common pitfall of having no time or skills to analyze the data.

- **When will the report be ready for use?** Development and program staff collaboratively determine the reporting schedule. Development staff may need data and formal reports by a certain date to fulfill funder reporting requirements. Program staff may run internal reports on an ongoing basis to drive program planning. Both parties should discuss their needs and agree on a schedule that will work for both.

You may have a funder report is due in June when the program runs October through May. It may be tough to create a report only a month after concluding the program, depending upon program size and your capacity to analyze and report on the data. Program staff may be able to gather preliminary data to satisfy the funder.

This is why these two departments need to coordinate the reporting schedule: so everyone gets the data they need when they need them.

For timeline examples, please visit the companion website 💻: www.evaluationintoaction.com/getyourdata.

# CHAPTER 11

# Put It All Together

Now you have all of the pieces needed to put your evaluation plan together. A typical program evaluation plan includes the following elements:

1. Introduction (half page)
2. Program Description (one to three pages)
3. Methodology (one to three pages)
4. Logic Model or Impact Model (one page)
5. Measurements (one to two pages)
6. Next Steps, Timeline, and/or Recommendations (one page or less)

The following sections outline each element of the plan, using excerpts from two evaluation plans:

- Northwest Housing Alternatives Resident Services program (NHA)
- Candlelighters for Children with Cancer Family Camp program (Candlelighters)

# Introduction

The introduction provides general information about your program, your mission, and why you're doing a program evaluation. It may seem unnecessary, but if you have staff turnover or need to bring a board member up to speed, the Introduction provides a needed overview before diving into the details.

## Example: Introduction (NHA)

*Northwest Housing Alternatives (NHA) provides afford-able housing options for families, seniors, and people with special needs across 1,546 households in Oregon. The NHA Resident Services program is an on-site program dedicated to connecting residents to resources and providing assistance.*

*Currently, the NHA Resident Services (RS) program tracks outputs such as the number of service requests, number of programming events, and number of food boxes delivered. These outputs are important to track; however, they do not provide information on program implementation or impact. This plan outlines how impact, as well as implementation, will be evaluated. Two key activities informed this plan: (1) document analysis, and (2) evaluation planning session with staff members.*

## Example: Candlelighters Introduction

*Candlelighters for Children with Cancer provides support for the whole family battling pediatric cancer throughout their entire journey. They offer a community of support by bringing healing, hope, and light to families. One of the primary and most popular programs is the annual Family Camp.*

*Candlelighters seeks to implement a comprehensive evaluation process for its Family Camp program to measure the degree to which the program is meeting its goals and to identify areas for growth and improvement. This evaluation plan will serve to identify the Family Camp program goals and activities, align them with measurable outcomes, and describe the methodology for collecting, analyzing, and reporting data to assess program impact as well as program implementation efforts.*

## Program Description

The program or project description section provides more details about the program itself. It details what the program is, who it serves, and how it is delivered. There can also be some history as to how the program came to be as well as any current evaluation efforts.

### Example: Program Description (NHA)

*The overall goal of the Resident Services Program is to **connect** residents to services that promote housing stability. The Resident Services Program includes one program director and six resident service coordinators (RSC) across thirty-one properties for low-income populations. The 2,600 residents may fall into one or more of the following groups:*

- *Seniors: Residents who are fifty-five years or older*

- *Families: Residents who have one or more children under the age of eighteen living with them*

- *Individuals with special needs: Residents who have mental and/or physical disabilities*

*RSCs visit properties approximately once per week. Activities vary from direct services, such as eviction prevention/notice intervention, to coordinating on-site events with partner organizations, such as budgeting classes or nurse visits.*

## Example: Candlelighters Program Description

*For more than eighteen years, Candlelighters has held a Family Camp program at Camp Harlow in Eugene, Oregon, over Labor Day weekend. This three-day weekend camp brings together families from throughout Oregon and Southwest Washington who are unified by the shared experience of pediatric cancer.*

*This program builds a network of community that provides emotional and practical support. Families are provided a respite from the daily stresses of cancer treatment as they participate in a variety of fun and inclusive traditional camp activities and recreation with others who are experiencing similar challenges. The camp weekend is provided free of charge to all families who choose to attend.*

*To date, the Family Camp program has served more than four thousand family members. Each annual camp session includes the following participants:*

- *Families (80)*

- *Volunteers (8–10)*

- *Healthcare Providers (2)*

- *Candlelighters Staff (4)*

*Some families have attended Family Camp for a few years, while others are new. To welcome new families, Family Camp staff select families with previous attendance to be host families. They are families who have attended camp for at least three years. They assist with welcoming new families at camp. This past year they were given additional responsibilities, including volunteering the first morning for registration, helping host the parent social hour, and greeting and talking with all new families. A few families also volunteered to help in other ways, including serving snow cones and mediating any conflicts at camp.*

*Candlelighters is looking to demonstrate measurable impact for its Family Camp program to earn grants and increase major-donor participation, as well as to provide direction for growth and improvement. An effective evaluation process relies on the collection of data that is meaningful and realistic for the program.*

*Candlelighters has been collecting some data on Family Camp, both quantitative and qualitative. They are currently working on a database solution to more efficiently combine these data for better reporting on impact and outcomes.*

*The quantitative data consists of participation numbers for families, years of participation in camp, volunteer hours, and demographics. Qualitative data has been recorded on the importance of family camp to participants and how it has helped improve and enrich their lives. These experiences are useful for telling the story of family camp and illustrating what camp means for each family. The balance of having both the numbers and the stories is a key element to understanding the program's impact and effectiveness. The collection of these experiences, together with the quantitative data, can be integrated into a formal evaluation framework.*

# Methodology

Methodology defines evaluation questions, program elements to consider, and measurable outcomes.

The Resident Services example is far longer than the one for Family Camp. Because of the complexity of the Resident Services program, it was necessary to provide more details in terms of stakeholders and the frequency of various activities, and to address housing stability. None of these concepts were explained in their previous documents, so the evaluation plan is an opportunity to connect these dots and to align concepts leading up to the impact model.

The differences between these programs illustrate how you can frame your program overview in the evaluation plan. Take into consideration how to articulate what your program does, who is involved, how the program is delivered, all leading up to your impact or logic model.

### Example: Methodology (NHA)

The discovery process for the NW Housing Alternatives Resident Services program revealed different stakeholders, which affected the implementation and, therefore, the impact of the program. For example, a property manager oversees each property, and the resident service coordinators (RSCs) need to coordinate services with them. This relationship was not articulated in their original materials. In discovery, it became clear that the methodology needed to include this group as a part of the program delivery model as well as a group to gather data from. Because the methodology was long, we included data visualization to keep readers engaged.

*Methodology*

*The RS program is complex, with different levels of stakeholders and program services to consider. Also, the RS program is in the process of migrating data management from spreadsheets to a database. All of these factors influence the methodology to employ. These factors are explored to set the foundation from which the methodology will stem.*

*Stakeholders*

*Four stakeholder groups influence the RSCs' ability to fulfill their role. Primary stakeholders include property managers and service partner organizations that are involved with residents on an ongoing basis. Secondary stakeholders include case managers and off-site family members who are involved sometimes and with some, but not all, residents. Their influence on the RS program is described below.*

| Primary Stakeholders | Relationship to RSC |
|---|---|
| 31 Property Managers | Help or hinder |
| 69 Resident Service Partners | Collaborative |

**Property Managers (PM):** *The role of the property manager is to oversee the property and ensure that residents follow the property rules. However, the disposition of the person in this role can help or hinder the RSCs' efforts.*

*PMs can help the RSCs' efforts by collaborating before notices are issued to better understand why the resident is breaking rules. They can also help by remaining calm when a resident is upset, working with the RSC to resolve any challenging situations.*

*PMs hinder RSCs' efforts by engaging in conflict with residents. RSCs frequently facilitate conflict mediation between property managers and residents. In another example, PMs hinder RSCs' efforts when they issue notices without checking in with RSCs or residents first. For instance, if a PM issues a notice based on rules not being adhered to, such as playing music too loudly, the RSC may find out the resident simply fell asleep with the music on and did not intend to break a rule.*

*The evaluation plan focuses on measuring the implementation and impact made by the RS program; therefore, the issues regarding the relationship between the RSCs and property managers is separate from the evaluation. Since property managers vary widely in their approach to their role, NHA may consider a facilitated process to strengthen the RSC/PM relationship. This process establishes a team approach that promotes housing stability.*

**Service Partners:** *RSCs collaborate with an estimated sixty-nine partners to ensure residents' needs are met. Primarily, seventeen partners are used regularly, while the remaining* *fifty-two are used on an as-needed basis (see Appendix A for complete list). RSCs identify residents' needs and coordinate with partners to meet those needs. For example, if food insecurity is an issue, RSCs may contact Sunshine Division to provide food boxes.*

*Each property is unique in needs, depending upon the population group served. For example, properties that serve families need RSCs to coordinate youth engagement programs, whereas properties that serve seniors need RSCs to coordinate assistance from aging and disability agencies.*

| Secondary Stakeholders | Relationship to RSC |
|---|---|
| Case Managers | Communicate |
| Off-site Family | |

**Case Managers:** *Some individuals have a case manager to help with their situation. The RSC's role is to communicate with the case managers as needed. However, it is the case manager's primary job to manage the overall care for these individuals.*

**Families:** *Some residents have family living in the area who can also serve as a means of support. RSCs may coordinate social activities and/or other events to welcome family visits and strengthen family relationships. In this case, communication with these off-site family members is also the nature of this relationship.*

### *Program Services*

*NHA's thirty-one properties all differ in terms of resident types/needs and, therefore, the types of services provided. Services vary in terms of delivery, frequency, and residents' housing stability status.*

*RSCs provide services directly as well as coordinate services with service partners. Illustrative of the complexity of this role, service delivery is separated into two delivery types, as follows:*

- ***Direct Services:*** *Provided by RSCs to residents, typically for residents who are at a higher risk of losing housing.*

- ***Coordinated Services:*** *RSCs identify what is needed and then coordinate that service with one of sixty-nine service partners. These services are provided for residents across the housing stability spectrum.*

*Frequency affects evaluation activities because the dosage of each service may influence the impact of services on housing stability. Service frequency may vary from daily to less than once per month. In the evaluation planning session, RSCs identified each of the nineteen services as occurring daily, weekly, bimonthly, monthly, or less than once a month. Results showed that frequency varies across properties.*

*The figure below illustrates that RSCs agree 63 percent (twelve) of services belong in one or two frequency categories. For example, some RSCs reported emergency food services occurred daily, while others reported a weekly occurrence. Therefore, a new category of daily/weekly was created for reporting purposes to better understand service frequency.*

| RSC's agree on frequency of 63% of program activities | |
|---|---|
| **Daily** | • Eviction Prevention<br>• Health and Wellness |
| **Daily/Weekly** | • After school activities<br>• Benefit programs<br>• Emergency food services<br>• Health care options<br>• Notice prevention |
| **Weekly/bimonthly** | • Social events |
| **Bimonthly/monthly** | • Employment services |
| **Monthly** | • Food stamps<br>• IDA program |
| **< 1x per month** | • Tax information |

*The remaining seven services spanned across different frequency categories. For example, budgeting classes occurred for some RSCs every week. For other RSCs, it occurred less than once per month. This lack of consistency across properties is important to consider when evaluating the implementation and impact of the program. Services that occur more frequently are likely to have the most influence on program impact; therefore, the evaluation will measure the impact and effectiveness of services that occur daily and/or weekly.*

*Housing stability is also a factor in terms of evaluation, exploring the questions:*

- *What services support residents in different situations?*

- *How do services differ for residents who are at higher risk of losing housing compared to those who are at a lower risk?*

*A housing stability scale defined five categories in which residents may fall, ranging from 1 (low risk of losing housing) to 5 (high risk). RSCs identified where program services fell within these categories. For example, social events are an activity associated with a low risk of losing housing, whereas eviction prevention is an activity for people at high risk of doing so. A separate housing stability scale will be developed and tested with all staff.*

*The methodology addresses the following key evaluation questions:*

1. *What impact does the RS program have on residents?*

2. *How effective is program implementation?*

*The key to successfully implementing this program is that the RSCs are the liaison between residents and the fulfillment of their needs. To address the evaluation questions, the specific change expected to occur has been broken down into specific expected outcomes, as follows:*

- **Create** *a community within each property.*
  *Through social events and on-site programs, RSCs cultivate a culture that reduces isolation and promotes community. The assumption is that if a resident feels connected to a community, they are more likely to remain housed there.*

- **Improve** *support.*
  *Many residents have struggles such as mental health difficulties, physical disabilities, and/or lack of support from friends and/*

*or family. The RSCs strive to support residents to help them feel that they are not alone and have a place to ask for help.*

- **Decrease** *negative behavior that can result in conflicts; reduce the eviction rate.*

  *Negative behavior, such as lack of lease compliance, can put residents at risk of losing their housing. RSCs may work directly with residents to reduce their negative behavior and, ultimately, reduce the eviction rate.*

- **Increase** *knowledge in identified areas of need and/or interest. The direct and coordinated services increase knowledge in areas of need (e.g., food security) as well as interest (e.g., financial education).*

- **Increase** *understanding of notice prevention and lease compliance. RSC's most frequent service across all properties is helping residents understand notice prevention and lease compliance. By understanding these two areas, residents are more likely to adhere to the lease rules resulting in fewer notices issued.*

- **Increase** *self-sufficiency.*

  *Overall, the RS program can cultivate self-sufficiency for residents. Helping residents understand how to secure food, legal assistance, and other services can help teach them how to do these activities for themselves.*

*The expected outcomes drive the content of all data collection tools. They are important change statements, clarifying what exactly the RS program expects to change as a result of program implementation. A program impact model is a visual summary that captures the relationships between program goal, services, outcomes, and measurements.*

### Example: Methodology (Candlelighters)

*For the Candlelighters Family Camp program, the discovery process revealed a gap between how activities were presented and the impact staff members said the camp had on participants. This section explained how the gap was revealed and what it meant for the program evaluation plan. We worked collaboratively with staff members to ensure the new program framework resonated with them before finalizing the methodology to measure the outcomes.*

*The document analysis and stakeholder survey revealed a gap between the camp activities and what staff reported as the impact of Family Camp on the participants. The camp activities included, for example, swimming, crafts, and family movie night. Program impact described by staff consisted of statements such as, "Lessen isolation and depression;" "Create a source of strength;" and "Gain support for entire families." The disconnect between the activities and outcomes led to the question: How do these types of activities relate to the significant impact identified by the key stakeholders? More importantly, why do some of the camp participants share that if they knew that this is what camp would be like, they would have participated much sooner? These questions highlight a need to further define the Family Camp program.*

*The identification of this gap led to the development of a new framework for the program model that effectively links the activities and impact. It's not just the activities that are important in Family Camp; it's the conversations and interactions that happen during the activities themselves. Active participation in the Family Camp activities contributes to each individual's social, emotional, and learning needs.*

*The variety of camp activities offered throughout the weekend provides the opportunity for participants to self-select the degree to which their own social, emotional, and knowledge needs are met during camp. Family Camp participants include all ages, diverse roles (for example, parent, child, or sibling), and are at different points along the cancer journey (newly diagnosed to bereaved). As a result, each participant will have unique needs. While all camp activities offer opportunities for connection and conversation, they present a spectrum from very contemplative activities, such as the meditation workshops, to more interactive, such as the parent social hour. Regardless of where each activity lies on this spectrum, all camp activities are conducive to forming a network of support and the creation of a community of people who share the common experience of pediatric cancer. Family Camp is about being with others who are sharing your journey with cancer, but allows for participants to choose what they need at that particular point in their journey.*

*Families come from different geographic regions and engage in activities that build a community support system. The act of (1) bringing people together from different geographic regions, and (2) offering engaging activities in a safe space provides the opportunities to connect socially, emotionally, and thoughtfully.*

*The activity-to-impact gap can be closed by inserting the following outcome categories. These categories further define the program itself in terms of overarching areas:*

- **Social:** *Activities that promote interaction and having fun.*

- **Emotional:** *Activities that help create a coping framework for this journey.*

- **Knowledge:** *Activities that promote sharing lessons and learning from each other.*

*The outcome statements below align to these three categories, illustrating how change is expected to occur across three different areas as a result of Family Camp participation:*

- *To expand **social connections** with other families experiencing pediatric cancer.*

- *To establish an **emotional** coping framework.*

- *To increase **knowledge** about how to navigate the medical process and financial resources.*

*Alignment is a critical ingredient in an evaluation design. Alignment throughout the mission, program goals, activities, and outcomes ensures evaluation activities are measuring what matters. This new framework links the activities, outcomes, and impact of the Family Camp program while also aligning the Candlelighters mission and the goal of the Family Camp program by incorporating the element of community to tie all of the pieces together.*

**The goal of the Family Camp is to create a community support system that will improve the overall quality of life for families experiencing pediatric cancer.**

*The goal illustrates the intent of the program as it fits within the organization's mission statement.*

**Our mission is to provide a community of healing, hope, and light throughout the life-long journey of childhood cancer. We advocate, we educate, we build partnerships, and we foster solidarity for all families experiencing cancer.**

*The impact model illustrates the new framework for the Family Camp program.*

## Impact or Logic Model

This summarizes all of the information presented in your plan so far. Either impact model or logic model should be a full-page full-color depiction of your program and its expected outcomes. See Chapter 8, Create Your Logic or Impact Model, for a refresher.

For full-page full-color impact models, visit the companion website 💻: www.evaluationintoaction.com/getyourdata.

## Measurements

This section details what data collection tools you plan to use to measure outputs and outcomes to show your program's effectiveness and impact. These include surveys, interviews, focus groups, tools for monitoring and tracking program activities, and other measurements as appropriate. It is important to write them all out to confirm that everyone is on the same page about what data will be collected and from whom.

## Example: Measurements (NHA)

The NW Housing Alternatives Resident Services program measurements section had two parts: Program Implementation Measurements and Impact Measurements. During the evaluation planning process, they were also adopting a new database. This was great timing to migrate from using paper forms and spreadsheets to moving all their data collection tools to the new database.

The Program Implementation section includes ways that evaluation data can be used. This illustrated the value of adopting the evaluation process, which was time-consuming in the beginning but became a part of their day-to-day operations. It helped the staff see exactly how evaluation data could help them manage program activities more effectively.

### *Measurements*

*A multifaceted approach will address the outcomes in the program impact model. Upon approval of this plan, data collection tools will be completed.*

*Given the amount of data to collect, NHA should consider hiring a data coordinator. This person would oversee all evaluation activities, helping RSCs where needed. The data coordinator would also establish relationships with property managers and gather move-in/move-out rates monthly. This role would lighten the RSC's workload and move the RS program toward an efficient, realistic evaluation system. A common guideline for program evaluation is to budget at least 10 percent of the program's operating budget toward program evaluation, which can be taken into consideration in creating this new role.*

### Program Implementation: Ongoing Data Collection Activities

- **Intake:** *When a resident first requests a service, complete this intake to create an initial record. The intake will include resident name, property, groups, key demographics, service requested, and housing stability rating. More information about this rating is provided below.*

- **Service Form:** *This form includes the most frequent service activities (daily or weekly) that RSCs implement. These are conflict mediation with the tenant, conflict mediation with the property manager, eviction prevention, notice intervention, health/wellness, benefit programs, emergency food services, food boxes delivered, and after-school activities.*

- **Event Attendance (social event, health fair, class, etc.):** *Document event, event type, topic, length, who delivered it, and attendance.*

- **Move-in/Move-out across All Properties:** *Data coordinator for all properties to check in with property managers monthly to track eviction rates, move-ins and move-outs. These data will be updated in the database.*

**Housing Stability Rating:** *For each participating resident, a baseline stability rating is recorded by the RSC. Once the database is implemented, ratings will be updated every fifth service request to record if ratings are changing. The database will be programmed to remind the RSCs when the stability rating update is due.*

### *Housing Stability Rating Descriptions:*

*1 (Low Risk) = Residents who are stable. They are more independent than other residents, employed, and seeking growth opportunities.*

*2 = Residents who are in a more positive space, seeking growth opportunities but still needing help accessing resources and encouragement to attend social events.*

*3 = Residents who have their basic needs met yet may experience other struggles, such as unemployment and/or poor health. They require assistance to ensure they remain housed and continue to have essential needs met.*

*4 = Residents for whom basic needs, such as food and clothing, are not being met.*

*5 (High Risk) = Residents who have received notices, evictions, and/or have conflicts with property managers/other residents. These circumstances put them at high risk of losing housing.*

### *Process Evaluation: Examples of how potential data may be used*

*The service form is key to measuring implementation as it gathers detailed data on the services provided as well as their frequency. Program services may be changed rapidly based on data that are collected and analyzed. For reporting, the data coordinator can also analyze the number of residents who improved their housing stability rating over a specific period, indicating positive trends.*

*The RS program is in the process of selecting a database, which will make it easier for staff to input, manage, and use data. Some examples of data that can be analyzed and then used include:*

***Potential finding #1:*** *Number of notice preventions by the resident. Some residents may show a high number within a short period.*

> ***Action:*** *May intensify services to ensure housing stabilizes, connect with case manager if applicable, or other actions to stabilize housing.*

***Potential finding #2:*** *Number of residents who have moved up at least one housing stability rating over a three-month period.*

> ***Action:*** *May be ready to invite them to the Individual Development Account (IDA) program or other growth opportunities. See if they are willing to mentor or host new residents or those who are in the 1 or 2 housing rating.*

***Potential finding #3:*** *Number of residents who have required food security services. Look for residents who have needed these services an unusually high number of times.*

> ***Action:*** *Connect with their case manager, property manager, and the residents. Look for wrap-around services to understand what is underneath the ongoing food security needs.*

***Potential finding #4:*** *Number of conflict mediations between property managers and residents by site.*

*Action: For the properties with an unusually high number of conflict mediation activities, NHA may need to alert the property manager's supervisor to resolve the issue.*

### Surveys: Impact Evaluation

*The easiest method to gather data from multiple stakeholders is a survey. These surveys will be administered on an annual basis by the data coordinator.*

- *Resident Survey: This survey will assess the impact the program has had on the residents and gather the following data: (1) demographics, (2) which activities they participated in, (3) helpfulness of those activities, and (4) the overall impact of the program for them. All impact-related items will align with the outcomes.*

- *Property Manager Survey: This online survey will identify what property managers think of the program and how they believe it is impacting residents. Specific survey items will align with the outcomes.*

- *Service Partner Survey: This online survey will gather what partners think about program impact and implementation. Specific survey items will align with the outcomes where applicable. We will determine if the survey will be administered to primary partners or all partners.*

## Example: Measurement (Candlelighters)

The Candlelighters for Children with Cancer Family Camp monitors program activities through surveys with children, teens, and parents. All three surveys address the same outcomes while taking differences into consideration. First, these three groups have slightly different activities. For example, teens participate in Teen Social Hour, children participate in Arts and Crafts, and parents can attend Parent Social Hour and meditation workshops.

Differences in language ability must also be taken into consideration. Young children have different reading abilities compared to teens or adults. Surveys may measure the same things for adults and children, but items must be presented differently on surveys to be understood by each audience.

Notice how measurements are aligned across all data sources: children, teens, parents, and staff. All surveys address the outcomes from their impact model, ensuring questions about each outcome are asked of all data sources.

### Measurements

*A multifaceted approach will be employed to address all the outcomes in the evaluation model. By evaluating the outcomes and understanding how they impact the Family Camp participants, Candlelighters can then better understand which outcomes are being met and which are not. The following are the recommended measurements.*

***Activity Attendance.*** *Each session leader will complete an attendance form for each session and each day. Tracking activity attendance will provide a comprehensive picture of how many people attended each session. Camp activities that best facilitate connections and/or conversations will be more popular and, therefore, demonstrate greater attendance numbers. The data will inform future programming by identifying the camp activities that most align with the achievement* *of the program outcomes. Activities that are sparsely attended may not have as much success in achieving the intended objectives of creating connections and facilitating conversations due to low participation.*

***Camp Participant Survey.*** *Administer paper surveys at the end of each camp weekend. The request for participant feedback should be included in the camp schedule, so people know about it in advance. Since language skills vary among the different age groups of camp participants, several versions of the survey will be created. Three surveys that will address the same outcomes will be developed for the following groups:*

- *Parents/Caregivers*

- *Teens (13-18 years)*

- *Children (8-12 years)*

***Service Provider Reflection Survey.*** *Staff, volunteers, and health care providers will complete a brief survey at the end of camp as well. This can be an online or a paper survey, depending upon the anticipated response rate. The purpose of the survey is to understand the effectiveness of program implementation as well as to obtain feedback on the overall impact as it aligns with the measurable outcomes.*

## Next Steps, Timeline, and/or Recommendations

The last section describes the next steps to implement the plan. This may include a timeline with recommendations on how to move forward. A timeline is important to ensure the reporting schedule will fulfill both program and development staff needs. For some programs, a timeline is not needed. Rather, details on what action steps are needed to implement the evaluation plan. The following examples illustrate these two scenarios. For NHA, their program is complex and includes multiple people. Therefore, a timeline was necessary. Candlelighters Family Camp, on the other hand, is a three-day program and didn't require a detailed timeline. Rather, they needed an outline of the next steps to implement the plan.

## Example: Recommendations and Next Steps (Candlelighters)

### Recommendations and Next Steps

*One of the gaps identified in the development of this evaluation plan was the need for a better description of Family Camp so that families could really understand what Family Camp entailed and the benefits of their participation. Families expressed that if they knew that this is what camp would be like, they would have participated much sooner. This evaluation plan succeeds in providing a more refined program description as well as aligning the program activities and outcomes to the Family Camp program goal. These concepts have been presented here in clear language as well as in a visual model.*

*It is suggested that Candlelighters use the information in this plan across all departments when talking about the Family Camp and promoting the program. This includes all development, communications, and program staff. For example, grant proposals related to Family Camp should use the program goal, core activities, and outcome statements that are presented in this plan. Program staff should use these elements in their program materials when inviting families to register for camp.*

*Further, it is suggested this evaluation plan be presented to the board, with an emphasis on how to talk about Family Camp moving forward. This recommendation will ensure consistent messaging about Family Camp across all board and staff members, as well as to all families and stakeholders. This common messaging for Family Camp should extend through all Candlelighters' communications, including the website, marketing materials, proposals, and correspondence.*

## Example: NHA Timeline and Next Steps

The NHA timeline and recommendations provide an overview of what work will be completed by whom and by when. One staff concern was that program evaluation would take too much time. This timeline helped alleviate these concerns by providing clear expectations about their role in the evaluation process.

For timeline examples, please visit the companion website 🖥 : www.evaluationintoaction.com/getyourdata.

This last section puts the final piece into place. Now you have everything you need to create your program evaluation plan. Remember, collaboration is key. Before moving on to create data collection tools, work with your team to ensure the plan is meaningful and realistic. Avoid pitfalls by making sure everyone agrees to what will be collected, by whom, and when. A written plan that's agreed to by the entire staff helps ensure evaluation success.

Part Three explains how to create surveys and other data collection tools and processes. This is the first step to implementing your program evaluation plan.

*Resident Services Program: Evaluation Activities Workflow*

| Measurements | Data Collection | | Manage | Analysis/Report | Communicate | Use |
| --- | --- | --- | --- | --- | --- | --- |
| | Who will collect | How it will be collected | | | | |
| Intake Form | RSCs | Tablet | Database | Director or Data Coordinator | Director, Data Coordinator, and Executive Director | Program staff to inform program planning Development staff to support fundraising efforts |
| Service Activity form | | | | | | |
| Event attendance | | | | | | |
| Move-in/ Move-out | Data Coordinator | Phone or in person | | | | |
| Annual Resident survey | Data Coordinator and RSCs | Paper survey administered in person | Data entered by the data coordinator or intern | | | |
| Annual Partner survey | Data Coordinator | Online | Online survey tool | | | |
| Annual Property Manager survey | Data Coordinator | Online | Online survey tool | | | |

## Part Three

# COLLECT YOUR DATA

Now that you have an evaluation plan in place, it is time to collect data on program implementation and impact. You'll start by creating data collection tools, such as forms and surveys.

Your outputs and outcomes drive the design of your data collection tools. As we saw in Chapter Five, Align Planning with Reporting, outcomes and outputs define what you expect to see change. The data collection tools then align to the same outputs and outcomes.

For example, if you expect families to build life skills, your data collection tools should measure that. If you expect increased interest in math, your data collection tools should measure that.

Every nonprofit is unique. Setting up a system to collect data depends on staff availability and expertise to gather, manage, analyze, and report on the data. This book focuses on these two data collection methods:

- **Program data management** is a standardized approach to gathering data on program participation and services delivered, also called *outputs*. These data are critical not just for reporting on participation, but can also help define program direction.

- **Surveys** are a cost-effective way to gather data. They can gather process evaluation data and impact data anonymously for information on program impact and implementation.

While other methods like focus groups, rubrics, and other more advanced techniques may require technical training or outside expertise, this book is designed to help you start managing program data and conducting surveys right away.

CHAPTER 12

# Manage Program Data

It's important to create a system to gather, manage, analyze, and use program data. They are often gathered at the most basic level: the demographics of those served and the number of activities delivered. As previously discussed, most program-related data are outputs, meaning "bean counting" activities. How many people participated? How many activities did you do? What came out of the program in terms of numbers?

Continuous program evaluation can help you better understand how to streamline processes for more efficient use of resources, including how staff can use their time and how your dollars can go further.

Common types of program data include:

- **Background data**, including demographics, history, and other information gathered from participants.

- **Activity delivery**, including activity type, frequency, and length. It is important to track what you are actually delivering to understand how well you're meeting program goals.
- **Participation**, meaning the number of participants for each interaction. This could include attendance at trainings or meetings with a case manager. Having a system to gather participation data across your program activities will facilitate evaluation.
- **Rating scale** to standardize how the staff is monitoring success toward program goals.

It's important to establish a process for gathering and entering data. Take the time, in the beginning, to set this up to avoid stress down the line. By being clear upfront who's doing what, you'll avoid the situation where one person says, "I thought you were tracking attendance," and the other person says, "No, I thought *you* were tracking it."

### Questions to Consider

- What questions do you want to answer from the data?
- What dashboard reporting views would be most helpful to drive action on a daily, weekly, monthly, quarterly, and annual basis?

## Background Data

If your program requires an application, intake form, or some other form of paperwork before participation, this is the opportunity to gather data for evaluation and reporting purposes. It's much better to do this upfront, and less work down the line. That way, you don't have to go back and try to get it later after the program is completed.

Common background data include age, gender, education level, income level, occupation, ethnic background, race, and marital status.

You can add program-specific items to your intake form to help with evaluation. For example, the NHA Resident Services Intake form below focuses on demographics as well as which of the three groups the resident is in. Collecting these data upfront saves time and makes reporting easier down the line.

Only ask for demographic data if you need it for program improvement, securing funds, or reporting. If you don't use it, don't spend resources collecting it. Most of the time, gathering demographic data in your initial intake process is enough. You don't want to overwhelm your participants with paperwork by asking for demographics every single time.

## Example: Intake form (NHA)

### NHA: Resident Services Program Resident Intake Form

RSCs complete this form in their database when a resident requests their first service. Information may be gathered from the resident as well as the property manager.

| Item | Response |
|---|---|
| Date of request | MM/DD/YYYY |
| Resident name | (Open field, enter name) |
| Property | (Drop down menu) |
| Group | Senior: 55 years old or older |
| | Special Needs: physical or mental needs |
| | Family: living with one or more children |
| | Individual: no kids, no special needs |
| Number in household | 1<br>2<br>3<br>4<br>5 or more |
| Race/ethnic background | African American/Black |
| | Asian/Pacific Islander |
| | Bi-racial/Multi-racial |
| | Caucasian/White |
| | Latino/Hispanic |
| | Native American |
| | Other (specify): |
| Gender | Cisgender male<br>Cisgender female<br>Transgender male<br>Transgender female |
| Date of Birth | (MM/DD/YYYY) |
| Household Income | ($enter amount) |

| Item | Response |
|------|----------|
| Income Source | Employment<br>Social Security<br>Pension<br>Child Support |
| Housing Stability Baseline Rating | 1 (low risk)<br>2<br>3<br>4<br>5 (high risk) |

Housing stability baseline rating was a system developed as part of the program evaluation process as a tool for RSCs to track how housing stability changes (or doesn't change) for each resident over time.

As described in the concept paper "Program Evaluation and Data Culture in Resident Services" by Chari Smith and Julia Doty:

*The Housing Stability rating scale allows us to assess stability based on requests for services, program participation, lease violation notices, etc. RSC directly performs assessment based on these factors after the first service request, then every three service requests after that OR every six months. This allows us to establish a baseline, change over time, and create an end point for those residents who only need one intervention. Assessing housing stability over time allows us to offer the appropriate intervention to each household.*

## Questions to Consider

- What background data do you currently track?
- Any background data to add to or remove from current data collection tools?

## Activity Data

Tracking activity data helps you understand how often activities occur and the length of each activity. All of these are outputs of implementing the program. Some examples:

- *The tutoring program provides one-hour 1:1 sessions with students three times per week.*
- *Life skill classes are delivered twice per month and are two hours in length.*
- *100 food boxes delivered per month.*

Let's look at the first activity statement about the tutoring program. To get to that statement, staff had to document that following:

- **Program name:** *Youth Tutoring Program.*
- **Activity:** *A tutoring program for students who are reading below grade level in elementary school. One tutor meets with one student to build academic skills and confidence in their academic ability.*
- **Length:** *Each tutoring session is one hour.*
- **Frequency:** *Three times per week.*

Complete the following form to collect activity data so you can better understand program activities as a whole:

- **Program name:**
- **Activity:**
- **Length (hours, minutes):**
- **Frequency (times per day, week, month, year):**

### Questions to Consider

- What activities do you offer, including one-on-one sessions, classes, events, trainings, and other events?

- How do you track the activities you deliver in terms of length and frequency?

## Participation Data

Participation data measures how many people are participating in your program. Hopefully, you are already tracking this in some fashion, whether on paper or in a spreadsheet.

If you have a single activity, you can track participation through registration online or at the event. Or you may have a large program with multiple activities. Tracking participation for each activity provides valuable information about which activities are well attended and which are not.

Decide who will document the number of participants and how. Also, make sure to designate who is responsible for entering participation data into a spreadsheet or database.

For an event, designate a staff member to create and manage a sign-in sheet to track attendance. For a class, make sure the teacher takes attendance by jotting down all the names or simply counting up the number of people in the room.

When reporting out, you can easily calculate the total number of participants across all classes. For example, the report may state: "We offered five classes over three months with an average of fifteen people attending per class."

### Example: Participation data (Candlelighters)

Candlelighters for Children with Cancer Family Camp tracked how many people attended the camp. They also offered different activities over the three-day weekend. They used the schedule, which included the length and frequency for each activity, to create tracking forms for each session leader to complete. The camp schedule excerpt below shows some of the activities they did.

*10:00 a.m.   Swimming*

*11:00 a.m.   Arts and crafts*

*12:00 p.m.   Lunch*

*1:30 p.m.    Parent meditation workshop*

The activity attendance form for each session included this information:

- *Name of activity*
- *Day and time offered*
- *Session leader name*
- *Number of participants*

Collecting these data enabled them to report on which sessions were heavily attended and which were not, providing insight into how to adjust session offerings for the following year.

## Questions to Consider

- Do you have a process to track who is participating in your program?
- Are there levels to the activities to factor into participation reporting?
- What other information do you need to track program participation?

# Rating Scale

A rating scale provides a standardized approach that all staff use to monitor progress toward goals. It's a great option when you have multiple staff members implementing the same program across multiple participants.

## Example: Rating scale (NHA)

In the NHA intake form, RSCs used a housing stability scale to track the stability of each resident's housing situation. For example, for residents at high risk of losing housing, the RSC could intervene with the property manager and resident to resolve the problem to enable the resident to remain housed. Alternatively, residents at a low risk of losing housing could benefit from an Individual Development Account (IDA) program to help them save money.

Before the rating scale, RSCs had no way of consistently understanding how activities promoted housing stability for each resident. The rating system provided ongoing data to take the guesswork out of what services to offer at a specific property or for a specific resident.

## Example: Rating scale (PHFS)

This example illustrates how tracking participation and creating a rating scale changed Portland Homeless Family Solutions' (PHFS) approach to program implementation.

PHFS provides comprehensive services to families that are homeless in Portland, Oregon. Shelter Coordinators worked with parents regularly to secure housing, offering classes in topics like life skills and budgeting, along with childcare.

Before engaging in program evaluation, they were already tracking:

- Number of families, adults, and children served
- Length of stay

To better understand the continuum of how a family participates in their program, it was important to track what PHFS activities they attended, such as life skills classes, meetings with their case managers, and attendance to other activities. This information helped the Shelter Coordinator better understand what families were doing or, more importantly, what they weren't doing.

As part of the new program evaluation system, attendance at all program activities was tracked and reviewed. This participation data helped them understand more about each family and how to help increase their engagement in the classes.

The discovery process revealed that families' progress toward getting housed was not standardized. If a Shelter Coordinator was out sick or left their job, it caused inconsistent information about the family's progress toward getting housed. In other cases, there just wasn't enough information tracked to understand why some families drop out of the program altogether.

This is a key element in process evaluation: using data on an ongoing basis to find breakdowns or success and facilitate improvement. For PHFS, a standardized process to use data helped them better track—and therefore understand—each family's needs to move them toward getting housed.

This meant creating a rating scale from *no housing* to *housed*. Shelter Coordinators helped families with many activities along that scale, including finding available housing, applying for housing, and securing housing but not yet housed. It was clear that tracking each family through this continuum, along with their participation in PHFS activities, helped shelter coordinators better understand how to get that family housed.

All of these data are outputs. When several people are involved with implementing the same program across multiple participants, as in this case, it is important to create a standardized system to collect data to improve program operations.

The following table shows the form all coordinators used to track where each family was in the process of getting housing. They used the data (outputs) to better understand what support the family needed to secure housing. Shelter Coordinators met at least weekly with families and used the form below to track data in their database.

*Portland Homeless Family Solutions: Housing Status Rating Scale form*

|  | Not started | Applying for housing | Secured housing but have not moved in (note reason) | Housed | Disengaged |
|---|---|---|---|---|---|
| Housing status |  |  |  |  |  |

## Question to Consider

- Can you use a rating scale to standardize how you are measuring progress toward program goals?

# Spreadsheets vs. Database

Now that you know what data you need to track, you need to decide how to manage data so you can successfully analyze and use them. This section outlines two primary tools for managing data: spreadsheets and databases.

Whether to use spreadsheets or a database really depends on your organizational capacity in terms of staff expertise, time, and funds. If you use spreadsheets, someone will need to oversee data entry and analysis. A database solution, on the other hand, typically has data analysis features built into it.

## The Case for Spreadsheets

If you aren't systematically tracking anything yet, a spreadsheet is a good place to start. This low-cost data management option is great for programs with few activities or participants. It does require you to have someone on staff with the skills to manage and analyze spreadsheet data.

A small nonprofit organization may want to focus on creating a realistic system using spreadsheets to enter and manage data. As your organization grows, put database solutions on your to-do list. It will reduce hours spent on data entry and analysis.

## Example: Participation spreadsheet (Youth Tutoring Program)

To track participation, the Youth Tutoring Program spreadsheet included the following information:

| Student name | Tutor | Session One | Session Two | Session Three | Total sessions |
|---|---|---|---|---|---|
| Mark Jones | John Smith | 1/15/2020 | 1/30/2020 | 2/15/2020 | 3 |

The project coordinator maintained the spreadsheet. Data were collected from tutors via email to confirm that sessions occurred. The last column tracking the total number of sessions lets the project coordinator see at a glance how many sessions were delivered over time. Tracking the names of students and tutors makes it easy to calculate how many students and tutors are involved with the program. Finally, tracking the session dates helps the project coordinator understand if tutors are missing sessions and to follow up as to why that's occurring.

## Example: Participation spreadsheet (Resident Education Program)

The following spreadsheet tracks data for a fictitious resident education program in an affordable housing community.

*Resident Education Program: Attendance to classes*

| Class name | Date | Length | Number of participants |
|---|---|---|---|
| Budgeting | 1/30/2020 | 60 minutes | 14 |
| Life Skills | 2/15/2020 | 60 minutes | 18 |
| Create your Resume | 2/28/2020 | 90 minutes | 17 |

## Questions to Consider

- Which types of data will you collect in the spreadsheet: background, participation, and/or activity data? For each, which specific data will be collected?
- Who will oversee data collection (typically the program coordinator or director)?
- Who will be responsible for entering data into the spreadsheet?
- Who will be responsible for analyzing and reporting the data? How frequently?

## The Case for a Database

Implementing a new program evaluation plan can be a great time to adopt a database solution. I am a fan of nonprofits getting out of spreadsheets and into a database as soon as possible. It's more expensive and time-consuming on the front end, but the payoff is transformative.

If you can swing the cost of a database solution, do that. It will save you so much time down the line because you can easily pull the data you need with a few clicks. I've never yet heard a client say, "I wish we didn't have this super-easy database solution to track and pull data from. I'd much rather spend hours tackling a spreadsheet."

## Why Switch from Spreadsheets to a Database

Justin Yuen, CEO of Grouptrail, shares common criteria that lead nonprofits to switch from spreadsheets to a database:

- *Needing to track a process toward achieving program goals across your work in addition to data relating to activities*

- *Addressing the complexity of juggling multiple spreadsheets to track participant-level data linked to numerous types of activities and programs*

- *Reduce the time required by data entry due to the user interface design of spreadsheets to find multiple places to record information*

- *Make it easier to generate and update template reports for numerous types of stakeholders who turn data into action on an ongoing basis*

- *Linking of data from multiple sources including spreadsheets and other systems*

- *Requirement of making access control, privacy, and security controllable by an administrator while restricting the sharing of the data*

- *Ability to easily view and report on historical data and progress notes*

## Design your Database

It's best to be clear on what data you want to track before selecting a database vendor. Having a list of which data you plan to track will make it easier to determine which solution is best for you.

You can help your vendor or internal database development team understand the organization's needs by creating a *database architecture*, which defines data to be collected and what users need to get out of the database.

For full-color examples of database architectures, visit the companion website 💻 : www.evaluationintoaction.com/getyourdata.

Justin Yuen, CEO of Grouptrail, who has worked with hundreds of nonprofit professionals to develop a visual, user-friendly database to manage their program data, has this to say:

> *Besides identifying the essential data fields you want to capture in the columns, and the different types of data types you want to track in the rows, it's helpful to come up with a list of key questions that it would be helpful to have answers for from a range of stakeholders that will define the reporting views needed. You can think of the above examples as the raw data being tracked in forms or sheets, and the reporting views as summary sheets and charts that will drive action.*

## Example: Database architecture (NHA)

NHA used Salesforce to manage their data. The new program evaluation plan included the following data collection tools:

**Intake:** *Resident background information and demographics*

**Services delivered:** *Services used*

**On-site events:** *The number of events, type, and number of residents that attended.*

These were all created as paper forms, making it easy for the database development team to understand what data to track. The key was to ensure the database was set up for the resident service coordinators to use the system easily.

We put staff in the driver's seat and mapped out on paper what the home page and following pages of the database would look like. This overview of the database architecture streamlined communication between NHA and the database development team:

**Database Home Page**

*Staff Login/password*

**What would you like to do today?**

- *Complete intake form for the resident new to services*

- *Complete service form for the existing resident*

- *Record on-site event*

- *Record move-in or move-out for the resident*

- *View upcoming housing stability ratings to record by resident and month*

## Example: Database migration (Grouptrail + CARA)

Ariela Friedman, Director of Strategy, Education, and Community Development at Grouptrail, shared this story of how Grouptrail assisted College Access: Research & Action (CARA) to migrate from spreadsheets to a database solution:

*College Access: Research & Action (CARA) has worked in over eighty public high schools in NYC since 2011 with the goal of ensuring that first-generation-to-college students, low-income students, and students of color have the knowledge and support necessary to enroll in and graduate from college.*

*As part of CARA's College Bridge program, coaches help graduating high school students matriculate into college. Originally, these coaches helped students with the twenty-eight tasks needed to complete the enrollment process, from filling out financial aid to submitting final transcripts. They tracked their work in Google Sheets for anywhere from one hundred to four hundred seniors per high school. In 2015, College Bridge expanded to a full year model, where coaches would now support the college application process in addition to enrollment, and needed to find a better solution to track the now seventy-plus tasks. CARA decided to move to a database for three reasons:*

- *Easy scaling: from tracking twenty-eight to over seventy-five tasks over a year.*

- *Saving counselors and coaches time as they are updating student records and identifying students who need follow up.*

- *Relieving the time and cost of manually creating reports for each school numerous times per year.*

*With Grouptrail, CARA developed a student-focused tracking tool that organized all of the necessary student tasks into four to-do lists: College Readiness, Applications and Admission, Financial Aid, and Enrollment. The database structure ensured continuity and consistency of the data as opposed to Google Sheets, where staff would reorganize columns, change column names, and add their own language to indicate the level of completion for a task. All of these differences made it very time-consuming and expensive to create reports and to get a timely snapshot of what was happening in the program.*

*The reports that CARA created with Grouptrail could be run with the touch of a button and without any additional investment in time or money. The reports were created as templates and would give you the latest information in the format you wanted, which eliminated the cost of running individual reports for schools. Where in the past CARA paid a consultant thousands of dollars for one or two school-specific reports per year, CARA could now run these reports monthly, for the same cost, and for a greater number of schools.*

*Using a database also allowed staff to identify trends, issues, and priorities in real-time. For instance, the program director was responsible for the administration of programing across thirty-plus schools, but could not see aggregate data from Google Sheets during the year (based on the issues listed above). When they transitioned to a database, the director could see what was happening in real-time and could identify success and challenges that needed to be addressed. A clear example of this is the tracking of financial aid applications. Coaches helped students complete three different financial aid applications and tracked all of them in their new database. In the early spring, the program director noticed the completion rate was significantly lower for one of the applications across multiple schools. The director followed up with coaches to see if there was really an issue or if it was a data entry error. The numbers were true, and through talking to coaches they were able to identify the root issue and make a plan to ensure that students completed all of the applications. In the past, the issue may have been uncovered in the yearly report, and then an intervention would have been identified in the following year.*

*Making a choice to transition to a database can be difficult because there are costs and staff time that you will incur. Similar to CARA, organizations often identify the need to transition to a database as they are going through other types of transition. Often scaling programs is a key pivot point. Scaling and other programmatic changes highlight how the challenges of a spreadsheet will grow exponentially with the growth of their program.*

## Select a Database Vendor

The process of selecting what database is best for your organization can be overwhelming. There are a lot of options at different price points.

Now that you know which data you want to track in a database, it is time to vet potential vendors, whether by working directly with database companies, engaging a database consultant familiar with nonprofit data management and evaluation, or working with a company that combines both.

## Questions for selecting a database vendor

Justin Yuen of Grouptrail shares tips on how to prepare before contacting a database vendor:

- **Identify priorities:** *What are your top three goals for improving upon your current tracking system?*

- **Describe user stories:** *What are the different staff roles that will interact with the database? What are their goals, and how will they interact with the database?*

- **Determine the budget:** *What is the budget for launch and yearly costs?*

- **Determine timing:** *When do you have time to take this on? When do you need to launch?*

- **Evaluate data migration needs:** *Do you have existing data that would need to be scrubbed and imported into the new system?*

- **Establish leadership:** *Who on staff is positioned to manage this project and related priorities?*

Key questions to ask when evaluating a vendor:

- *What is your annual licensing fee for the database platform?*

- *What is included in the annual licensing (server maintenance and hosting, ongoing feature updates, customer support, etc.)?*

- *Is consulting and training required, and what is the number of hours and cost for rolling out the database?*

- *How do you handle the migration of existing data?*

- *Can you set up a demo database based on your need and produce reports that are core to your data evaluation?*

Once you have identified two or three potential database vendors, ask for references from existing clients to provide important insight into which vendor is the best fit for you.

The following chapter details the basics of survey design, along with strategies to successfully administer surveys and real-world examples.

CHAPTER 13

# Design Realistic Surveys

Survey design can range from simple to complex. In this book, we will focus on descriptive analysis, which is a simple and straightforward way of tabulating responses that describe your population. Descriptive analysis counts responses to specific choices—for instance, 78 percent of survey participants responded yes.

Inferential analysis, on the other hand, looks at the relationships between variables, such as cause and effect. This type of analysis is more complex and requires training. If you want to go down this path, plan on hiring an outside expert to help. Otherwise, stick with descriptive analysis.

Surveys are generally administered during or at the conclusion of program activities. If your program is ongoing, choose a convenient point in the program cycle to administer surveys. This can coincide with the end of your fiscal year. Or, if development staff need to report data to funders by a specific date, make that the due date for your report and work backward from there. Development and program staff must create and agree to a reporting schedule together.

This chapter explains basic survey design, including survey administration, data management, analysis, and reporting.

## Survey Design Guidelines

Let's start with some ground rules regarding survey design. Before you dive into creating the content to measure impact, take these concepts into consideration:

### Open vs. close-ended items

Open-ended questions gather qualitative data by asking survey participants questions like, *What did you like best about our program?* and *What did you like the least?* These question types offer the opportunity to gather the stories from participants.

Two key open-ended questions to include in your surveys are, *What went well?* and *What needs improvement?* Depending on your program and your outcomes, you'll want to ask a third question: *What impact, if any, did this program have on you?*

Be sure to ask about both sides of the coin: both what they liked and what they didn't like. Another way to ask this is *What were the successes? What were the challenges?* Offering the opportunity for participants to freely describe both positive and negative aspects of your program provides insight into improvement opportunities and overall impact.

Close-ended questions require participants to choose an answer. As Sheila Robinson and Kim Firth Leonard describe in *Designing Quality Survey Questions*, a close-ended question includes a distinct set of response options. Response options are generally a rating scale with three to five choices.

## Example: Survey (Candlelighters)

Candlelighters for Children with Cancer wanted to know about the helpfulness of their Family Camp. The survey excerpt below illustrates two survey items from the parent survey.

| Please rate how helpful Family Camp was with the followinG areas: | Extremely helpful | Moderately helpful | A little helpful | Not helpful |
|---|---|---|---|---|
| Trying to maintain family stability | | | | |
| Emotional support from Family camp staff | | | | |

We weren't sure if we should use a scale based on helpful/not helpful, useful/not useful, or strongly agree/disagree. We created these mock statements for a final report to see what resonated:

*75 percent of survey participants felt the emotional support from family camp staff was extremely helpful.*
*75 percent of survey participants felt the emotional support from family camp staff was extremely useful.*
*75 percent of survey participants strongly agreed that family camp staff provided emotional support.*

We talked through these ideas. For the third one, it wasn't enough to know if emotional support occurred. We cared if it was useful or helpful. Ultimately, we decided that *helpful* was a better fit than *useful*. Since one of the outcomes was about feeling emotionally supported, it was better aligned with the outcome to measure how helpful the program was.

In addition, the literature review revealed an article, "CHIP Coping Health Inventory for Parents: An Assessment of Parental Coping Patterns in the Care of the Chronically Ill Child," by McCubbin, H. I., McCubbin, M. A., Patterson, J. M., Cauble, A. E., Wilson, L. R., and Warwick, W. published in the *Journal of Marriage and Family*. They measured how parents coped regarding what was *helpful* to them. Since this term was already tested, we went with *helpful*.

### Example: Survey (NHA)

NHA wanted to understand to what degree their services helped residents to improve in specific areas. As the survey excerpt below shows, the four-point scale includes three options for improvement and one for those with no opinion.

| Because of the Resident Services program ... | Improved a lot | Improved somewhat | Not at all improved | No opinion |
|---|---|---|---|---|
| Residents' connection to the community has ... | | | | |

## Ask about one item at a time

If you want to know how helpful, informative, and timely your training was, ask about each item separately. Asking about them together makes it hard for people to give a single answer. For instance, what if they strongly agreed it was helpful but disagreed that it was timely?

## Example: Too many items per question

| | Strongly agree | Agree | Neutral | Disagree | Strongly disagree |
|---|---|---|---|---|---|
| The training was helpful, informative and timely | | | | | |

Listing these as three separate items allows you to understand to what degree the training was helpful, informative, and timely.

## Example: One item per question

| | Strongly agree | Agree | Neutral | Disagree | Strongly disagree |
|---|---|---|---|---|---|
| The training was helpful | | | | | |
| The training was informative | | | | | |
| The training was timely | | | | | |

## Avoid leading questions

It is easy to frame a question in a way that leads participants to the answer you want. For example, the question *Did you like the training?* leads participants to respond *Yes.* You're feeding them the answer. Don't do that.

A better format is open-ended, where participants write in their answer: *How did you feel about the training?* Or it can be close-ended: *Please rate how you feel about the training: Very good, good, average, poor, or very poor.*

## Select the appropriate language for your participants

Take into consideration word choice, reading levels, and other language-related factors to ensure your survey participants understand what you are asking them. Program staff are best equipped to provide feedback on language to use. You may also need to translate your survey into other languages.

## Example: Appropriate survey language (NHA)

Here's one survey item from the NHA resident survey:

| Because of participating in the Resident Services program, I ... | Strongly agree | Agree | Disagree | Strongly disagree | No opinion |
|---|---|---|---|---|---|
| ... am more connected to the community here. | | | | | |

In a conversation with staff, the *Strongly Agree/Strongly Disagree* scale felt too formal. We discussed with staff members what would be a better way to frame the question to measure outcomes. We determined a three-point scale would be less overwhelming for these low-income residents: *better/same/worse*, with an option if they weren't sure. Here's the final resident survey:

| Please choose one response that best matches what you think for each statement. | Better | The same | Worse | I don't know |
|---|---|---|---|---|
| Because of the Resident Services program, my connection to the community is ... | | | | |

## Conduct a literature review

A literature review is a great place to start your survey design. In some cases, surveys have already been created to measure whatever it is you want to measure. Finding something that already exists can save you a lot of time and effort. This is a great project for a research or evaluation student at a local university.

Starting with your general topic, do a deep dive into journals, articles, and other resources to review published studies, tools, and data.

## Example: Survey literature review (In4All)

In4All wanted a pre- or post-survey design to measure these outcomes:

- Students will increase their interest in STEM-related careers
- Students will improve their attitude toward STEM-related subjects

A literature review revealed an article that addressed measuring student attitudes toward STEM: "Development of the Attitude toward Science in School Assessment and Its Use to Investigate the Relationship between Science Achievement and Attitude toward Science in School," by Dr. Paul German in the *Journal of Research in Science Teaching*.

We used this survey with his permission, which enabled us to use a published data collection tool that was already tested with students.

## Example: Survey literature review (Candlelighters)

For the Children with Cancer Family Camp program, we explored what surveys already exist for similar programs. The Family Camp is a three-day camp for families experiencing pediatric cancer. Their outcomes are:

- *To expand **social connections** with other families experiencing pediatric cancer.*
- *To establish an **emotional** coping framework.*
- *To **increase knowledge** about how to navigate the medical process and financial resources.*

We searched using Google and Google Scholar for the following phrases:

- *measures of social support in patients with serious illness*
- *coping with cancer social support system*
- *emotional support for cancer patients*
- *camp for children with cancer/illness/disability*

These searches led to evaluation reports from other camps that addressed similar outcomes, whose bibliographies led to more resources. These helped us develop the participant survey for Candlelighters.

## Questions to Consider

- **Who will conduct the literature review?** This may be someone on staff, a university student, or volunteer with research experience. This effort generally takes 10–15 hours for someone with experience. Whoever does it, be sure they document the resources they find in a bibliography.
- **What is your timeline for a literature review?** Assign one person to oversee the implementation of your program evaluation plan. This includes allocating time to complete the literature review.
- **What phrases best describe your program** to search for surveys administered in similar programs?

## Pilot the Survey

If possible, pilot the survey with a small number of past participants or staff members to ensure the questions are understandable. This will allow you to fine-tune the language before administering to program participants.

# Create Survey Content

Now that you know the ground rules, let's dive into the details on creating survey content.

Remember, use your outcomes to drive the content of your questions. This ensures you're gathering data you will use.

To avoid survey fatigue, try to keep surveys to no more than two to four pages.

## Title and Introduction

Include the program name and year in the survey title. You can also include a season or specific month if that's helpful—for example, *Resident Survey, Spring 2020*.

The introduction describes the purpose of the survey and assures participants that their individual information will remain confidential and anonymous.

To ensure confidentiality, do not ask for participants' names. This increases the likelihood that they will provide honest answers if they know it cannot be tracked back to them.

## Background

The background section asks for basic information, such as demographics. Sometimes this is the first section, but it can also be the last. It depends upon what section is the best "ice breaker." You want people to start the survey feeling that it will be easy to complete.

## Program Participation

These data provide context as to how participants engaged with your program. You may want to ask about length or frequency, or participation, types of activities, or role in the program. Examples include:

- For a school-related program: *What grade are you in?*
- For a home repair program: *How long have you lived in your home?*
- For a support services program: *Which activities did you participate in?* (List activities and have them select all that apply.)

When you do the analysis, you may decide to separate the data to compare impact for different groups. In a school-related program, you could compare grades nine and ten with grades eleven and twelve to see if there's a difference in responses regarding impact.

As always, think about what data you will use for funder reports or ongoing program improvement. For example, if you don't need demographics, don't ask for them. Only ask for what you need.

## Impact Data

These survey items relate to the measurable outcomes you defined in your evaluation plan. Outcomes are the foundation from which impact-related questions arise.

This is a great opportunity to include both close-ended and open-ended questions. Typically, you'd start with close-ended questions. Once they're warmed up, you can ask open-ended questions about what they liked and didn't like and the overall impact the program had on them. I've seen incredible impact stories as well as valuable information on how to improve come out of these simple questions.

In some cases, however, it may make more sense to ask demographics at the end of the survey. It depends upon your participants, and what your team determines would be the best order for the survey sections. If you're undecided, create two versions and test them out with a few past participants. Get their feedback before you roll the survey out to the entire group.

### Example: Survey template (training program)

Here's a template with survey sections for a training program.

*Training Program* ←——————— Title

Script

*[insert date]* ←——————— Timeframe

*We are interested in your feedback about our training program. This survey will help us understand what went well, what needs improvement, and overall impact. Your information will remain confidential and reported out anonymously.*

*Today's date: _____*

Background section

**Background information.** *We would like to know more about you. Please answer the following questions.*

**1.** *How old are you? (Circle one)*

    *a) 17 years or less*

    *b) 18–21*

    *c) 22–44*

    *d) 45–64*

    *e) 65 years or older*

*2. What best describes you? (Circle all that apply)*

    *a) American Indian or Alaskan Native*

*b) Asian*

*c) Black/African American*

*d) Native Hawaiian or Pacific Islander*

*e) White*

*f) Prefer not to answer*

*g) Prefer to describe: (open ended)*

3. *Are you of Hispanic, Latino, or Spanish origin? (Circle one)*

   *a) Yes*

   *b) No*

   *c) Prefer not to answer*

4. *What is your gender identity? (Circle one)*

   *a) Cisgender man*

   *b) Cisgender woman*

   *c) Gender fluid/gender non-conforming*

   *d) Non-binary/genderqueer*

   *e) Transgender man*

   *f) Transgender woman*

   *g) Prefer to describe: (open ended)*

5. *What is your sexual orientation? (Select all that apply )*

   *a) Asexual*

   *b) Bisexual*

   *c) Heterosexual/Straight*

   *d) Homosexual/Gay*

   *e) Homosexual/Lesbian*

   *f) Pansexual*

   *g) Queer*

   *h) Questioning*

   *i) Prefer to describe: (open ended)*

*Participation section*

**Program participation.** *We would like to know to what degree you have participated in our training program.*

*6. Have you participated in our trainings before?*
    *a) Yes*
    *b) No*
    *c) Not sure*

*Impact section*

**Program feedback.** *We are interested to know how the program did or did not impact you. Please **mark one** response per statement.*

**Rating scale**

Rating scales let people rate improvement on specific variables from better to worse.

| Because of the (insert program name) completed ... | Better | The same | Worse | Not applicable |
|---|---|---|---|---|
| Survey items that align with your measurable outcomes. | | | | |

**Open-ended questions**

Leave plenty of room, so people have space to respond. I generally use one page for these three questions with plenty of space in between.

**Your thoughts:** *We want to better understand what you liked and did not like about our program.*

*What went well?*

*What needs improvement?*

*Any additional comments?*

Here's an actual survey example from NHA. Notice how the different survey parts gather information about participation and background, as well as data aligned to their outcomes.

## Example: Resident survey (NHA)

*NW Housing Alternatives: Resident Services Program Survey*

*Resident Annual Survey 2017: [insert property name]*

*Today's Date: [\_\_\_\_/\_\_\_\_/\_\_\_\_]*

Script ←

*Take a few minutes to do the Resident Services Program Survey. When you turn in your finished survey, please also turn in a raffle ticket with your name and contact information. Prizes will be announced on June 28.*

**Program Participation**
We included the name of the RSC to help residents remember who was providing services for them.

**Part One**: *What Resident Services did you use? This may include events, classes, and/or help you received from the Resident Services Coordinator [insert name].*

## 1. What services have you used in 2016 to present? (Please circle all that apply)

a) Help making phone calls

b) Help with health services

c) Help getting items such as furniture, clothes, and diapers

d) Went to classes (examples)

e) Went to social activities (potluck, birthday party)

f) Food

g) Help getting a job

h) Help with my lease

i) Help with not getting evicted

j) Help with problems I'm having with other residents

k) Help with problems I'm having with the property manager

l) Participated in the Individual Development Account (IDA) program

m) Other: (please explain):

## 2. How often have you used one or more of the services listed above? (Please choose one answer)

a) 1-3 times per month

b) 4-6 times per month

c) 6-8 times per month

d) 9 times per month or more

## 3. Were these services helpful to you? (Please choose one answer)

a) Very helpful

b) Helpful

c) Somewhat helpful

d) A little helpful

e) Not helpful

> ## Impact section
> For each outcome in the evaluation plan, there is a survey item below.

↓

*Part Two: We want to know what you think about our program. For each statement below, please choose 'better, the same, worse, or I don't know.' Thank you!*

| Please choose one response that best matches what you think for each statement. | Better | The same | Worse | I don't know |
|---|---|---|---|---|
| a) Because of the Resident Services Program, my connection to the community is . . . | | | | |
| b) Because of the Resident Services Program, what I know about lease rules is . . . | | | | |
| c) Because of the Resident Services Program, what I know about taking care of myself is . . . | | | | |

| | | | | |
|---|---|---|---|---|
| d) Because of the Resident Services Program, what I know about getting things such as food, furniture, and other needs is . . . | | | | |
| e) Because of the Resident Services Program, what I know about taking care of others is . . . | | | | |
| f) Because of the Resident Services Program, the support I have from neighbors and my community is . . . | | | | |
| g) Because of the Resident Services Program, what I know about health and wellness is . . . | | | | |
| h) Because of the Resident Services Program, what I know about controlling my money . . . | | | | |
| i) Because of the Resident Services Program, I get along with others . . . | | | | |

**Background information**

We decided to gather background information after asking about impact. These
demographics align with those in the Resident
Services Intake Form.

**Part Three:** *Tell us about yourself.*

## 4. What age group are you in? (Please circle one answer)

a)  <18 years old

b)  19–29

c)  30–39

d)  40–49

e)  50–55

f)  56 or older

## 5. Gender (Please circle one answer)

a)  Male

b)  Female

c)  Transgender Male

d)  Transgender Female

e)  Nonbinary/Genderqueer

f)  Prefer not to answer

g)  Prefer to describe: _____

**6. What is your ethnic background? (Please circle all that apply)**

a)  Caucasian/White

b)  African American/Black

c)  Asian/Pacific Islander

d)  Latino/Hispanic

e)  Native American

f)  Prefer to describe: _____

**Feedback on the program**

These open-ended questions gathered impact data as well as process data. Residents were invited to comment in any way they want. In some cases, we received data on how to improve program implementation. Others shared a story demonstrating the program's impact on them.

**Part Four:** *Please tell us your thoughts on our program.*

7. *What is the best part about our program?*

8. *What can we do better?*

Closing instruction

Always provide instructions on what to do with a finished survey.

*Please turn your finished survey in to [name].*

*Thank you!*

You should now have a basic sense of survey design, including using measurable outcomes to drive survey content and literature review results to inform survey design.

Be sure the questions in the Background and Program Participation sections align with questions in your intake or registration forms.

Avoid the temptation to ask for information "just because." This takes up valuable space on the survey and adds time to data analysis. With your team, think through which data you actually need and will use.

### Worksheet: Survey design

Use these steps to create your survey:

1.  **Background:** Determine what you need to gather regarding the survey participants' background.

2.  **Program participation:** Since you are not gathering names, what program participation information do you need to ask?

3.  **Impact:** Start with a close-ended rating scale for survey items aligned to your outcomes. Toward the end of the survey, include open-ended questions.

For a downloadable survey design template, visit the companion website 🖳: www.evaluationintoaction.com/getyourdata.

## Administer the Survey

Surveys can be administered by telephone, mail, online, or in-person interview or handout.

Telephone and in-person surveys require staff to speak directly with program participants, which may introduce bias. An outside expert can help with these methods. Mailing surveys may be expensive and typically yields a low response rate.

*The response rate* is the number of surveys you receive compared with the number of surveys you sent out. For example, if you administer the survey online to one hundred people and receive twenty completed surveys, your response rate is 20 percent.

This book focuses on these methods:

- **Online survey programs** (like Survey Monkey or Fluid-Surveys) offer data analysis and reporting tools, though response rates tend to be lower for online surveys compared to in person.
- **Paper (in-person) surveys** tend to have a higher response rate since you can administer the survey in the context of program activities.

How to decide? If you have the staff capacity and resources to administer a survey in person, do that. It will likely get you a better response rate.

If you do an online survey, provide an incentive such as a raffle or a $50 gift card to increase your response rate. Even if you hand out a survey in person, you can still enter the data into an online survey program to take advantage of data analysis and reporting tools.

With the Candlelighters Family Camp program, for example, camp participants complete the paper survey before they go home. The parent survey response rate was 87 percent because they were required to complete it before leaving.

For a home repair program, on the other hand, residents in rural Oregon were given a paper survey, along with verbal instructions to complete it within a week and a stamped, addressed envelope. The response rate varied from 40 to 100 percent across the nine participating organizations.

Whatever survey method you use, you need ongoing project management to ensure data are gathered with the best possible response rate. I generally strive for a response rate of 60 to 80 percent. It depends on how accessible program participants are to being surveyed.

You can increase your response rate even before you send out the survey to participants. The discussion with stakeholders on when and how to survey participants is a critical one to ensure data are gathered from as many people as possible.

Take the time to identify who will oversee collecting the data, communicating with participants, gathering permission or consent forms if needed, and creating a standardized process for all staff to follow. The following sections provide details for each step.

## Manage the project

It is critical to establish project management protocols to ensure data are gathered as intended.

As I've said before—and I'll repeat it because it's crucial—one person should be assigned to oversee the implementation of program evaluation as a whole.

The project manager for data collection oversees that data are gathered as defined in your plan. Ideally, this is the compulsively organized person in your organization who loves details and timelines and can keep the rollout moving. This person makes sure everyone is doing their agreed-upon job to gather data. A detailed timeline is discussed and agreed upon by everyone, and the project manager makes sure everyone sticks to the timeline.

## Communicate with participants

Be sure to set the expectation that participants are expected to complete a survey as a part of the program. This can take place in the intake or registration process with a statement like this:

*Thank you for being a part of [program name]. Your feedback is important. As a part of participating, you will be asked to complete surveys [say when], so we understand what is working, what is not working, and our overall impact. Thank you in advance for your time and insights.*

Other ways to communicate:
- Include details about the survey when you email participants with program details. Be sure to include when the survey will take place and how (in person or online).
- Send a letter along with any program materials.
- If your program involves live events, announce at the beginning that there will be a survey at the conclusion.

The key is to make sure participants know about the survey well before they actually receive it. By appealing to them beforehand, you have the opportunity to build awareness so they know what to expect.

## Example: Participant communication (NHA)

NW Housing Alternatives administered surveys to property managers, service providers, and residents. To communicate with them about the upcoming survey, they took the following steps:

- Sent an email to all property managers and service providers from the director, emphasizing why NHA was doing the survey, why their feedback was important, and when to expect and complete it.
- Flyers were posted in the properties informing residents when the survey would occur and that they'd be entered into a raffle for completing it.
- When resident service coordinators were at the properties, they let both property managers and residents know the survey dates and personally inviting them to provide valuable feedback.

## Get permission

Getting permission is such an important piece of the process that Kelly Jarvis and I wrote *Evaluation Mini-Guide #3: Permissions and Confidentiality.*

## Excerpt: Permissions and confidentiality

*How do we receive permission to conduct the evaluation and for students to participate?*

**Organizational Permission.** *You may be required to secure authorization or permission from the school board, another governing body, board, or person in your organization to conduct the evaluation. If you plan to conduct data collection* *activities on school grounds or during school hours, for example, permission from school personnel may be necessary. Investigate and follow the procedures for receiving clearance for evaluation through your organization and any partner organizations involved in the data collection processes. To request organization permission (or participant consent, described below), you will need to assemble and present information about the evaluation, such as:*

- *The rationale for conducting the evaluation (i.e., why it is important to do);*

- *What data will be collected (what questions will be asked) and from whom;*

- *When, where, and by whom data will be collected, entered, and stored;*

- *Potential risks and benefits to participants;*

- *Steps you will take to protect the confidentiality of participants; and*

- *How the results will be used.*

***Participant Consent.*** *In addition to securing any necessary organizational permissions, you must also obtain individuals' consent to participate in the evaluation. Once informed about the evaluation, adults from whom you plan to collect data—such as parents, teachers, or program staff—can provide consent for themselves. Depending on the extent of the data collection activity and any overarching requirements, such consent can be obtained either verbally (e.g., acknowledgment* *is given at the beginning of a focus group) or in writing (e.g., via a formalized consent form).*

*Collecting data from individuals under 18 years of age (e.g., students) typically requires parental permission. Parental consent procedures vary across school districts and can be either "active" (a student cannot participate in the evaluation unless their parent signs and returns a form to authorize participation) or "passive" (all students participate unless parents sign and return a form to disallow their child's participation). In either case, a student is not allowed to take part in the evaluation—that is, you cannot collect or use any data for that child—unless parental consent has been obtained according to local protocols. A sample parental permission form (for "passive" consent) is included in this mini-guide:*

### Sample Evaluation Permission Form

The Oregon Arts Commission has contracted with NPC Research to conduct an evaluation of [your program's name]. The evaluation will examine the program's functioning and impact, including what students like and don't like about participating in the program and whether their participation impacted their perceptions of art, school, college, or their career. If your child participates in the evaluation, they will be asked to complete two surveys, one at the start of the program and one at the end. The surveys will inquire about your child's exposure to/interest in art, experiences with the program, and desires for completing high school and college. The surveys will take about fifteen minutes to complete. In addition, the evaluation will collect information on your child's engagement in the program, as reported by the artists.

Participating in the evaluation will cause little or no risk to your child. One potential risk is that some children might find certain questions to be sensitive. We will protect your child's privacy by not disclosing your child's name to anyone outside of the program and not connecting their name to any survey answers. Data will only be reported in the aggregate; names will not be used. Though your child may not directly benefit from participating in the evaluation, the study results will help improve programs dedicated to the arts in Oregon for your child and other children in the future.

Participation in the evaluation is voluntary. If you decide you would not like your child to participate in the study, they can still take part in the arts program. Your child may also skip any questions in the surveys and may stop taking the survey at any point without penalty. If you would like to see the survey, please contact us for a copy.

Please read the section below and check the box only if you do NOT want your child to take part in the evaluation. If you check the box "no" below, sign this form and return it to us and your child will not participate. If you do not return the form, your child will be asked to participate. If you have questions about the evaluation, please contact the researchers [evaluator name, affiliation, phone number, email].

Thank you!

Your child's name: _____

I have read this permission form and I understand what the evaluation is about.

[    ] No, my child may not take part in the evaluation.

If you do not check this box, your signature provides permission for your child to participate in the evaluation.

Parent's signature: _____
Date: _____

For a sample permission form you can use, visit the companion website 🖥: www.evaluationintoaction.com/getyourdata.

## Train Staff

If multiple people are administering the survey, holding a group training with written procedures for data collection is essential to ensure that surveys are administered the same way no matter who does it.

## Example: Staff Training (NHA)

The NHA Resident Survey was administered in person by the six resident service coordinators across 31 properties. How can we make sure the survey is administered consistently across all properties?

A group training with written instructions on how to administer surveys made sure all staff collected surveys consistently and successfully. We agreed on a two-week timeframe in which all RSCs administered the surveys in person at each location. The written instructions included the same script each RSC would use, regardless of if they were administering it in a group setting, such as a pizza party, or going door to door. That way, all residents received the same instructions.

## Questions to Consider

Use these answers to create your successful data collection process:
- What groups will you create a survey for?
- Who will create these surveys, and by when?
- Who will be the project manager?
- How and when will you communicate the expectation to complete surveys to participants?

- Do you need permission to gather data?
- Do you need to train staff and/or create written instructions on administering the survey?

Congratulations! You've collected the data you need for program evaluation reporting. The next part outlines how to roll up your sleeves and dig into your data to create compelling reports to demonstrate your organization's impact.

## Part Four

# CREATE YOUR REPORTS

Now it's time to analyze your data and compile key messages from the findings into easily digestible and usable reports.

Formal program evaluation reports of the past were filled with text and tables and could run to several hundreds of pages. Thankfully, times have changed.

This book focuses on two simple reports that can demonstrate impact and accountability clearly and compellingly for both internal and external stakeholders:

- **Program Summary Impact Report**: A two-page summary loaded with graphics and key messages that demonstrate impact to the public.

- **Key Findings and Action Plan:** This lists key findings to inform program improvement to be shared with staff, board, and funders as appropriate.

If you need a more complete and formal report to satisfy a funder reporting requirement, you may need to retain a professional evaluator.

To create these reports, you'll need some basic skills in data analysis for quantitative and qualitative data. Once the data are analyzed and organized by outputs and outcomes, with successes and challenges highlighted, you'll compile them into internal and external reports.

These chapters guide you through the basics of data analysis and reporting for outputs and outcomes, as well as how to identify key findings and compile them into an action plan.

CHAPTER 14

# Data Analysis Basics

Okay, so you've collected your survey and program data, which is aligned to clearly defined outputs and outcomes. Now what? To create compelling reports, you analyze the data and organize them by output and outcome.

This comes back to the critical concept of alignment. Your report is organized around the outputs and outcomes in your program evaluation plan. To recap, here's the alignment process from Chapter Five, "Align Planning with Reporting.":

## Program Evaluation Alignment Process

**Make your plan.** Determine what will change (outcomes) and what to measure (outputs).

**Get your data.** Create data collection tools to gather data aligned to outputs and outcomes.

**Create your reports.** Present insights on outcomes and outputs through supporting data.

This excerpt from *Evaluation Mini-Guide #6: Data Analysis and Reporting*, which I wrote with Kelly Jarvis, has been adapted to focus on the data analysis aspect.

**Qualitative data** *(e.g., stories and comments collected via interviews, focus groups, and open-ended questions on surveys) are analyzed and coded for commonalities and main emergent themes across respondents. When reviewing the responses, note common threads and repetitive themes.*

**Quantitative data** *(e.g., numeric data collected via surveys and archival records) can be analyzed in a variety of ways that largely depend on how you have collected and managed your data. Generally speaking, there are three types of quantitative data analysis: descriptive, correlational, and inferential.*

**Descriptive analyses** *involve procedures that "describe" your population. This includes frequencies (i.e., how often a response is endorsed by participants) and means (i.e., average scores). This can also involve comparing these estimates across different subgroups, such as girls and boys.*

**Online survey programs,** *such as Survey Monkey, feature basic data analysis and reporting tools that will compute many descriptive statistics automatically.*

**Spreadsheets,** *such as Excel, can also produce many descriptive statistics, but not automatically. The user must have the skills and knowledge to program and run appropriate formulas.*

This book focuses on using *descriptive analysis*, which means looking at the frequencies of different responses. Calculating frequencies is something anyone can learn to do, especially with online tools to make it easy.

This book is intended to give you practices you can implement on your own, so we're going to stick with descriptive analysis here. If you need to examine statistical relationships between variables (*correlation*), or measure cause and effect for your program (*inferential statistics*), you'll need to hire an outside expert.

Analyzing output data is straightforward number crunching, while analyzing outcome data requires a deeper dive. The following sections provide an approach and examples for both.

## Analyze Output Data

Outputs are numbers. If you track them in a spreadsheet, you can count them up. If you track them in a database, you can easily run queries on how many people participated in program activities.

### Example: Reporting outputs (PHFS)

Portland Homeless Family Solutions include outputs in annual reports to illustrate participation across their programs.

***Program Impact***
*378 services provided*
*279 households*
*1,053 kids and parents*

They also report on services delivered. For example, "*Our adult education program provided 312 hours of training.*"

### Example: Reporting outputs (Candlelighters)

Candlelighters Family Camp program reported on participants and staff delivering the program.

*Program participants. 262 family camp participants in 2019 Program delivery included six Candlelighters staff, two health care providers, and eight to ten volunteers.*

## Questions to Consider

- What are your outputs?
- Who will gather the numbers to report on those outputs?
- How frequently do you need to collect outputs to show impact and improve programs?

# Analyze Outcome Data

Outcomes help demonstrate the impact your program makes. Outcome data largely comes from surveys. Before getting into analyzing data by outcome, let's first address how to present the quantitative survey results.

Whenever I hear something like *95 percent of people felt the program supported their needs*, my question is 95 percent of what? One hundred people? Ten thousand people? If you knew ninety-five people felt this way versus 9,500, would it shift your perception? It would for me. This is an example of a naked number, something to avoid doing in your analysis and reporting of quantitative survey data.

A naked number = a percentage with no reference to the total number participating. Naked numbers can lead to taking information out of context. Dressed numbers provide a complete picture.

Here's how you dress your numbers. Always include the response rate as well as the total number of people surveyed in your technical reports. Always. Here's an example from NHA's technical report, illustrating the total number of people in each group that participated in the survey.

## Example: Reporting survey response rate (NHA)

*Survey Response Rate by Group*

| Group | Total (N) | Number of surveys completed (n) | Response rate |
|-------|-----------|--------------------------------|---------------|
| Property Managers | 20 | 18 | 90% |
| Service Partners | 18 | 9 | 50% |
| Residents | 765 | 379 | 49% |

This provides a critical context to understand who exactly is giving feedback. If you pull any information from a report and include it in a summary report, grant proposal, marketing material, or anything else, dress your numbers. Here's an example of a dressed number – *ninety-five out of one hundred people surveyed felt the program supported their needs.* By adding *out of one hundred people surveyed,* the number is dressed. Now you know and have the context that out of one hundred, ninety-five felt the program supported their needs.

When you report survey data in your summary report, include a footnote with the response rate or the total number of people completing the survey. Too much information within the report itself can be distracting. A footnote provides the survey response details to give a meaningful context. NHA's program impact summary report included the following:

## Example: Survey data reporting (NHA)

The opening paragraph of the report:

*Methodologies included surveys to residents, service partners, and property managers. (Footnote notation.)*

*Footnote: Survey response rates are as follows: Property managers, 90% (n=18); Service partners, 50% (n=9); Residents, 49% (n=379).*

This means that 90 percent, or eighteen people, completed the survey. It provides the context of how many people are giving feedback in each group surveyed. In short, numbers are completely dressed.

Let's move on to analyzing the survey data. To start, fill in the entire survey with the frequencies for each item, and list all open-ended responses by question. This synthesizes all of the responses in one place, prepping you to organize data by the outcome.

Calculate both the frequency and percentage for each survey item, listing the number of responses first followed by the percentage in parentheses. This gives you a quick snapshot of both actual numbers and percentages. Both are important. Online data analysis programs can calculate percentages for you.

## Example: Survey synthesis (Candlelighters)

Ninety-four parents attended the Candlelighters Family Camp. Of those, 82 completed the survey, yielding a survey response rate of 87 percent. The internal report summarized parent survey results, and the number of surveys received—82—is the number used throughout the report to dress the percentages.

For *Strongly Agree,* the value is *45 (55 percent).* This means 45 parents strongly agreed that they made new friends, representing 55 percent of all parents who completed a survey.

Notice the column labeled *Missing.* If someone skipped a question, that response is counted as *Missing.*

*Family Camp 2019 Parent Survey excerpt (N=82)*

| As a result of participating in Family Camp, I made new friends I would have otherwise never met | | | | | |
|---|---|---|---|---|---|
| Strongly agree | Some-what agree | Neutral | Some-what disagree | Strongly disagree | Missing |
| 45 (55%) | 22 (27%) | 9 (11%) | 2 (2%) | 3 (4%) | 1 (1%) |

The open-ended comments are an entirely different story. To set up qualitative data analysis, take these steps:

1. List all comments beneath each question on a separate page or document.
2. Read through them, looking for common threads.
3. On a separate page or document, create categories as they arise.
4. Go back and code the comments that belong to each category.

## Questions to Consider

- Did many people say they liked one or two specific things the most?
- Is there a common thread as to what they liked the least?
- What comments show that a given outcome has or has not been met?

If there are no common threads, that is also important information to include in the report. You might include something like this in the introduction: *There was no general agreement on what went well. Comments ranged from X to X topics. Some specific comments are included below.*

When including comments, never include identifying information. Make sure the comment will not reveal who the person was that said it. Anonymity and confidentiality are crucial, always—no exceptions.

## Organize Survey Data by Outcome

Now you have a sense of how to do basic survey analysis, it is time to organize your data by the outcome. The data for each outcome illustrate the degree of progress made to fulfill them. This goes back to the concept of alignment. You'll restate each outcome and present quantitative and qualitative data that align with it.

### Example: Present data aligned with outcomes (NHA)

*One of the outcomes for the Resident Services program was to improve support for the residents they serve. Resident and Property Manager surveys both asked about this outcome. Take a look at how the data are organized.*

*It starts with restating the outcome, then provides quantitative and qualitative survey results that show progress toward this outcome.*

**Outcome: Improve support**

*Many residents have struggles such as mental health difficulties, physical disabilities, and/or lack of support from friends and/ or family. The RSCs strive to support residents to help them feel that they are not alone and have a place to ask for help.*

*Many managers felt this area improved (76 percent). Almost half (46 percent) of the residents reported support from neighbors/community improved because of the Resident Services program. However, residents commented on the support provided by the RSCs specifically. This suggests the improved support mostly stems from the RSCs, and, to a lesser degree, perhaps the neighbors and community.*

*Residents provided positive comments on the support provided by RSCs. Specific comments are as follows:*

*"It means a lot that there is someone that you can contact with problems. That is the most important thing: to be able to find help."*

*"Willingness to listen and provide assistance as necessary, and communication assistance with management."*

*"Support that is compassionate, and I am treated with respect. Someone to answer emotionally charged questions—helps me stay calm."*

*"I think it's very helpful. If you can't get around because of health problems, you don't have to worry about things getting done. The RSC is here to help with that. It means a lot to not have to worry because help is right downstairs."*

Did you see the alignment? It started with the outcome, followed by quantitative data from both the manager and resident survey results. The open-ended feedback showed how supported residents felt. Four responses were included in the final report to demonstrate how numbers and stories align with this outcome.

## Example: Present data aligned with outcomes (In4All)

In4All STEM Connect™ program evaluation included pre- and post-surveys with fourth-grade students, with quantitative responses alongside open-ended feedback aligned to each outcome. This report synthesized student pre- and post-surveys over three years.

### *Outcome: Students will increase their interest in STEM-related careers*

*Survey results over the last three years show interest in STEM-related careers improved specifically for a subset of students that were neutral or negative toward math or science in the pre-survey.*

### *Over the last 3 years, a total of:*

*94 students that had negative or neutral interest in science in the pre-survey increased their interest in science-related careers*

*159 students that had negative or neutral interest in math in the pre-survey increased their interest in math-related careers*

### *Students Speak:*

*"Awesome, I love it." (2017)*

*"When I grow up, I want to be a vet that includes math and science." (2016)*

*"I would love to have a job in science when I grow up." (2015)*

The In4All report used the same formula as the NHA report: state the outcome, then report the quantitative and qualitative results that support it.

## Questions to Consider

- What qualitative data do you have to report on your outcomes?
- What quantitative data do you have to report on your outcomes?
- What did you learn about program impact?
- Did the data reveal any areas in need of improvement or where there's great success?

Once you have completed basic data analysis, you can start compiling your reports. More data analysis techniques are woven into the following chapters, as data analysis and reporting go hand in hand.

# CHAPTER 15

# Create the External Report

The Program Impact Summary is a high-level, two-page report designed to quickly inform readers what the program is, how the evaluation was conducted, and what the results were by outcome or output.

Include both numbers and stories in your Program Impact Summary to give readers a snapshot of your program's impact.

This report leverages data visualization to communicate key findings. Start by sketching out a summary of what to include. Then move into adding graphic design treatment to make your summary pop, aligning report colors with your organization's brand colors.

For full-page, full-color examples of a Program Impact Summary Report, visit the companion website 💻: www.evaluationintoaction.com/getyourdata.

## Example: Program Impact Summary Design Concept (NHA)

The following example illustrates the design concept for the NHA Resident Services Program impact report. The resident services director and I collaborated on determining what content is most relevant to share with the public.

Notice how the report provides an overview of what the program does, including the number of people delivering it and receiving it, as well as specific activities. The second page presents data by outcome, including both quantitative and qualitative data demonstrating the degree to which the outcome was fulfilled. The balance of stories and numbers provided a holistic snapshot regarding each outcome.

*Northwest Housing Alternatives (logo)*
*Resident Services Program*
*Program Impact Report 2017*

*Northwest Housing Alternatives (NHA) creates opportunity through housing for seniors, families, and/or individuals with special needs. NHA's Resident Services Program connects 2,400 residents across ten counties to services that promote housing stability. Each property is unique in needs, depending upon the population group served. For example, properties with families need access to asset-building opportunities, whereas properties that serve seniors need access to resources that promote healthy aging and socialization. To meet these needs, each property is assigned a resident services coordinator (RSC) who visits that property approximately once per week. In 2017, Evaluation into Action conducted an independent*

*evaluation to understand the impact on residents. Method-
ologies included surveys to residents, service partners, and
property managers (insert footnote reporting the number of
surveys received).*

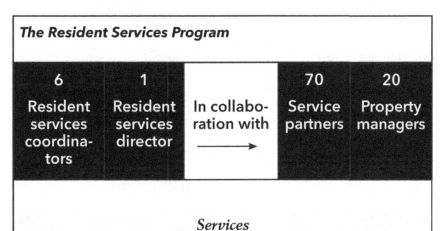

**The Resident Services Program**

| 6 | 1 | In collaboration with → | 70 | 20 |
|---|---|---|---|---|
| Resident services coordinators | Resident services director | | Service partners | Property managers |

### *Services*

*Eviction Prevention. Notice intervention/lease compliance.
Conflict mediation with other tenants and/or property
managers. Individual Development Account (IDA)
Program. Social events. Health & Wellness Programs
(Clinical nurse visits). Financial Education. Homework
clubs. Youth engagement.*

*Assistance: food, emergency food boxes, legal, employment,
transportation, rent, utility, childcare resources, tax.*

| Property Managers | |
|---|---|
| | "The RSC fills a critical role that is often overlooked at low-income housing projects of helping people succeed as residents of a community. |
| 89 percent report that Resident Services increases residents' ability to stay housed. | This includes helping residents understand lease violations, appropriate conduct, and other things that seem obvious to those of us lucky enough to have always had housing, but not so obvious to those who have spent a considerable amount of time on the streets." |
| **Residents** | |
| 93 percent report the Resident Services Program is "helpful" or "very helpful." | "It means a lot that there is someone that you can contact with problems. That is the most important thing: to be able to find help." |
| | "The listening ear. The monthly food. The answers to issues that come up with the willingness to sincerely help." |

### *Results*

Now that the first page of the report defines what the program does and some of the basic findings, the second page answers the question—what impact did the program have? Notice how this content aligns with the outcome, supported by both quantitative and qualitative data. So you have a balance of the numbers and the stories.

*Resident Services Program Impact*
*2017 Highlights*

*"I think the resident services program is crucial to promoting housing stability and offers a fantastic resource to residents so that they can feel informed, comfortable, and dignified in their home." Service Partner*

**Improved understanding of how to access resources.**
*RSCs provide a clear path for residents to learn how to access resources to meet their needs. This may include resources such as utility assistance, furniture, and/or hygiene products. This empowers them to better care for themselves through the help of the resident services coordinators.*

| | |
|---|---|
| Property managers (83 percent) and residents (53 percent) report improved understanding of how to access resources because of the Resident Services Program. | "Connecting us with the people that help pay our electric and gas bill and helping us with clothing and other resources in the community (is one of the best things about the program)." (Resident) |

**Stronger communities**. *Social events are a key service provided by the resident services coordinators. The events cultivate a culture that reduces isolation and promotes community. The assumption is that if a resident feels connected to a community, they are more likely to remain housed.*

| | |
|---|---|
| Residents (60 percent) and property managers (73 percent) felt their connection to the community is better because of the Resident Services Program. | "The events and programs that have been made available to use are not only very informational but fun also. I also feel more connected to the community in general." (Resident) |

**Improved Food Security**. *RSCs work with a range of service providers to ensure residents have access to food. This may include food boxes on a regular basis, farmers' market-style events in the common area, and/or emergency food assistance.*

| | |
|---|---|
| Residents (54 percent) report using food assistance and property managers (67 percent) report it has a great impact on residents. | "I just have to go down to the RSC's office and tell him to include my name on the month's list, and I'm assured of food. It helps a lot." (Resident) |

*How can we improve?*

*"Be available more" was a common response to this question. Many property managers and residents expressed increasing the RSCs' availability on-site would improve the program. As one property manager stated, "It might be easier if the*

*RSC wasn't spread so thin between so many buildings." In response, the NHA Resident Service Program is exploring how to increase RSCs' on-site availability in the future.*

*Special thanks to our residents, community partners, and property management partners for providing invaluable feedback so that we can continually administer the most effective Resident Services Program possible.*

The NHA program impact summary report is a full-color, two-sided document used to communicate the difference their program makes to key stakeholders. The following example from Candlelighters uses the same formula.

## Example: Program Impact Summary (Candlelighters)

The Candlelighters for Children with Cancer Family Camp program impact summary report followed this same formula. It starts with describing the program, participation, and the second page provides an overview of qualitative and quantitative data that align with the outcomes.

***Candlelighters for Children with Cancer: Family Camp (logo)***
***2019 Program Impact Summary Report (design concept)***

*The goal of Family Camp is to create a community support system that will improve the overall quality of life for families experiencing pediatric cancer. In 2019, Evaluation into Action conducted an independent evaluation to understand impact on families in terms of making social connections, establishing a coping framework, and increasing knowledge in how to navigate pediatric cancer. Methodologies included surveys with parents, teens, and children, as well as tracking attendance to activities and a staff debrief form at the conclusion of camp.*

Remember to always include the number of surveys completed by the group as a footnote. In this case, the footnote would come right after the last sentence, and includes the following:

*Parent surveys (N=82), teen surveys (N=40), child surveys (N=37), and staff debrief forms (N=15).*

The next section provides an overview of what the program is and who delivers it. This is the same exact graphic as in their impact model.

The participation numbers are also included on the first page, as follows:

*Results: Participation*

*262 Family Camp participants*

*Most (68 percent) were returning families to camp.*

*Most (72 percent) families have been dealing with pediatric cancer for four years or more.*

*Activities with the most participation: campfire, family photos, pool, and family movie night.*

*Activities liked the best: pool, zipline, horse rides, go-carts, family movie night, parent social hour.*

*"I liked playing in the splash pad with friends." (Child)*

*"I met several other families who are struggling through*

*difficult times with cancer. It was inspiring to see their positive outlook on life in spite of challenges." (Parent)*

The participation section starts with the total number of participants, followed by returning families and length of time dealing with pediatric cancer. The activities are highlighted next in terms of most participation and most popular. The two quotes provide balance to the numbers presented, illustrating a full snapshot of participation in terms of numbers and stories.

Like the NHA report, the Family Camp report's second page also focuses on the outcomes, providing the quantitative and qualitative results that align with each outcome.

*Results: Impact*

*Outcome: To expand social connections with other families experiencing pediatric cancer. Results show Family Camp expanded social connections for these families, as illustrated by the following:*

*90 percent of parents strongly agreed they spent time having fun with their family. "Seeing my daughter engage with other kiddos going through or [who] have gone through what she is going through. Boys got to be boys and play. Parents got to know other parents. Felt like we weren't so alone. We got to be a family."*

*Most children (95 percent) reported they had fun, and some (68 percent) reported they made new friends. "Happy to make new friends, sad to go home."*

*Seventy-three percent of teens report they enjoyed the social activities at family camp, and 40 percent said they participated in more social activities than they normally have time to do. Several teens commented that "being with friends" was most impactful to them.*

*Outcome: To establish an emotional coping framework. Survey results show Family Camp fulfilled this outcome to varying degrees. Highlights include:*

*Eight-seven percent of parents found Family Camp extremely helpful to get away from home-care tasks and responsibilities for some relief. As one parent commented, "Stress-free weekend!"*

*Eighty-nine percent report Family Camp was extremely (63 percent) or moderately (26 percent ) helpful in providing emotional support from other Family Camp participants. "In my community, there are no resources to meet other families impacted by pediatric cancer. This camp gave us a chance to realize there are others with the same experiences. Our children were able to meet kids who have been through what they have. It was such an amazing time."*

*Most teenagers and children agreed (43 percent, 57 percent) or somewhat agreed (43 percent, 19 percent) that Family Camp was a safe space to share their feelings. As one teenager shared what was most impactful over the weekend, "Getting to communicate to others in the same situation."*

*86 percent of children and 90 percent of parents felt they got to spend time with their family having fun. One child stated, "It was fun, relaxing, being with Mommy."*

*Outcome: To increase knowledge about how to navigate the medical process and financial resources. Results show less progress was made toward this outcome.*

*Twenty-seven percent of parents report they did receive advice on how to navigate pediatric oncology. Of those, 32 percent felt their understanding of how to do this increased a lot, while others (36 percent) felt it increased somewhat.*

*Ninety percent of parents report they did not receive advice from others on financial resources available.*

*Most families were returning to Family camp and/or have been experiencing pediatric cancer for four years or more. Therefore, this outcome may be relevant to families new to family camp. Since this includes a smaller group of people, Candlelighters may consider omitting this outcome from future formal program evaluation activities and instead conduct a small focus group with new families to better understand how their needs were met.*

*In summary, Family Camp creates a support system for families experiencing pediatric cancer, providing them with connections and conversations that will sustain them through this difficult period.*

## Questions to Consider

- How do you describe your program?
- Who participated in your program? If your program is continuous, how frequently do you report participation (monthly, quarterly, annually, etc.)?
- What data will you report by outcome?
- Who will complete the design concept?

- Who has the graphic design skills to complete the final report? This may be someone internal or an outside expert.

In addition to data related to outcomes and outputs, your data likely revealed your program's challenges and successes. The next chapter explains how to document these in a report intended for internal eyes only.

# CHAPTER 16

# Create the Internal Report

The Key Findings report celebrates successes and pulls out insights to inform program improvement. Output and outcome data may be included here, along with detail on how the data can inform program change. The purpose of this report is to gather relevant data to inform program improvement so it can be easily shared and discussed with key stakeholders.

## Example: Key Findings report (In4All)

In4All conducted surveys with these three groups:

- **Students:** Pre- and post- surveys were conducted to measure outcomes.
- **Teachers:** Surveys were conducted in January (mid-program, also called formative) and June (end of program, also called summative).
- **Business volunteers:** These were volunteers from STEM-related businesses who were trained to implement the

In4All STEM curriculum in fourth and fifth-grade class-rooms. They completed formative and summative surveys on the same timeline as the teachers.

Based on the teacher and volunteer 2016 summative survey results, a three-page report was generated titled *Key Findings to Improve Program Design*. The report was shared with program staff and volunteers. The following excerpt highlights a key success, informing In4All staff that a positive relationship was established between the teachers and volunteers.

*Outcome #1: Positive relationship between teacher and volunteer will be established.*

*Teachers (92 percent) and volunteers (83 percent) reported the working relationship between themselves and volunteers was either very positive or positive.*

*"When the STEM volunteers visited my classroom, they were so supportive and really seemed to enjoy teaching the kids the marble roll. It was good for me to see how they left the directions for the students open-ended, so the kids were forced to work together to figure out as a group the best way to create their marble roll design."*

*"Our volunteers were terrific! All three were originally from Mexico, and it was terrific for my Spanish Immersion students, particularly my Latin American students, to see role models of color. Thank you!"*

Notice how this report presents the outcome alongside survey results and comments that support quantitative findings. This was not included in the Program Impact Summary report because it was a lower level of detail, which informed program planning. Their public Impact Summary highlighted student impact, whereas data on program implementation was included in the internal report.

The internal report also highlighted areas in need of improvement. These came from analyzing the data looking for common threads. What did teachers say was working or not working? What did business volunteers say? Where did they overlap, and where were they different?

In the internal report, each key challenge was presented with an action step to resolve the challenge, large or small. Several challenges came up and were easily addressed by these action steps. For example, the following key finding gave In4All staff an action step to improve volunteers' first time in the classroom. Originally, business volunteers' first classroom visit involved them just talking to students, which is a missed opportunity for student engagement. Here's an excerpt from their internal report:

> ***Key finding. Introduction visit.*** *Some volunteers and teachers commented that it would be good to have a small activity for the first classroom visit.*
>
> ***Action.*** *In4All will provide an activity for the first visit that engages students.*

This is fairly small and simple. But tiny adjustments based on data add up to using ongoing feedback to make improvements that lead to greater impact.

NHA's program evaluation report also included what went well and what needs improvement. Like In4All teacher and volunteer surveys, the NHA resident, property manager, and service partner surveys also asked *What went well?* and *What needs improvement?*

Data analysis identified both successes and challenges. The following excerpt illustrates one of several successes so you can understand how to write this section of your internal report.

> *Service partner comments were overwhelmingly positive. This is consistent with the evaluation planning session results, illustrating the relationship between service partners and RSCs is collaborative. Some specific comments regarding what is working well include:*
>
> *"Excellent communication. Clear sense of needs and resources expected. Great staff coordination."*
>
> *"NWHA has been a valued partner agency of ours since 2013. The staff in the Resident Services are extremely professional, responsive, and go above and beyond to maintain a positive partnership with us. With their support, we are able to get diapering supplies into the hands of Oregon families that truly need them the most."*
>
> *"Our referral program with the Residents Services program is working well. It's a fairly simple and straightforward partnership—they send us referrals for their residents and we follow up with the residents directly."*
>
> *Residents also provided positive feedback. Some specific comments include:*
>
> *"I think your program is high minded and well-intentioned. The on-site workers I have met have been thorough and effective."*
>
> *"The whole program is amazing. I like everything about it!"*
>
> *"Just knowing that it is there and that I have someone to help with any problems is very comforting and stress-relieving."*

## Example: Key Findings report (NHA)

The NHA program evaluation revealed a number of challenges impacting program implementation. This excerpt highlights one of these challenges, followed by action steps to address the challenge.

*Both residents and property managers provided feedback on how the program can improve in specific areas. One was the need to improve communications in two different areas:*

*Lack of awareness about resident services offerings. As one resident stated, "There is so much about your program that I didn't know about until I got this questionnaire. I lived here at least nine months before I knew about the program's existence."*

*Lack of awareness about RSC's availability. As one manager stated, "Better time management. The residents have often sat here waiting for her to show up."*

*Both of these issues may be resolved through a strategic communications plan that includes activities such as a resident welcome packet, RSC's schedule posted on the property, and/or a resident mentor program.*

The data illustrated how communication was a challenge in two areas: program awareness and RSC availability. By highlighting these challenges first, followed by specific steps to improve communication, NHA worked toward improving communications in both areas.

In the final chapter, you'll learn about some ways to use your data beyond these reports.

CHAPTER 17

# Use Your Data

Once upon a time, the evaluation ended when the report was done. I had the good fortune to hear evaluation pioneer and author Dr. Michael Quinn Patton speak about utilization-focused evaluation. It completely changed how I approach program evaluation.

Dr. Patton believes that we should continue to work with organizations to ensure evaluation findings are used. He coined the concept of utilization-focused evaluation, which emphasizes that the use of findings is the whole point of doing evaluation. As he said in *Essentials of Utilization-Focused Evaluation*:

> ... *producing an evaluation report is not an end in itself. The purpose is to inform thought and action. Moving from what? to so what?, and now what?, means moving from data to interpretation to action. Action flows from using evaluation findings. Getting evaluations used is what utilization-focused evaluation is all about.*

211

This means that the fun has just begun once the reports are complete. Program evaluation reports are a springboard to demonstrate your impact and improve programs based on data. You can make good use of your data by communicating findings to keep key groups informed and inspired about what you're doing, and by using it for ongoing program improvement.

## Communicate Your Findings

Now that you have your internal and external reports, you can share back what you found to demonstrate your program's impact and how you can improve. What to share and how varies depending upon the audience. For example, your board may want more in-depth information than you share at your next fundraising event.

You'll want to create a communications plan outlining which data to communicate with which groups. This doesn't take a lot of time, but it does require clarity of intention. Here are some potential audiences for your evaluation data:

- **Board members** could get the Program Impact Summary, followed by a discussion on how data will be used.
- **Donors** could get a letter highlighting key findings, including successes and challenges and how challenges will be addressed.
- **Participants** might get a newsletter thanking them for helping with evaluation activities and sharing key highlights, along with any program changes that are relevant to them.

## Present Negative Findings

Sometimes the data show areas that truly need attention—more attention than you realized.

Don't panic. You're not alone. It happens all of the time. There's a way to manage negative findings that will benefit you and the community you serve. Don't try to sweep data under the rug from your funders. Instead, share how what you've learned will drive change.

This is easier said than done because you're passionate about your program and the difference you want to make. The last thing you want is for your data to show you're not making the difference you hoped.

But if you're not making the difference you thought you were, don't you want to know? If you view this as a learning opportunity and deflate the urge to hide negative data, you may be surprised how much learning and growth can come from the experience.

Meyer Memorial Trust is a funder located in Portland, Oregon. Program Officer Michael Parkhurst shares the value of nonprofit organizations being transparent about negative findings:

*Should people be honest with their funders? Yes. We want to understand what broke down and what we may be able to help with going forward. Was it a one-time hiccup or something beyond your control, like sudden changes in the economy? We try to break down the curtain of 'the great and powerful Oz.' I invite people to call me and tell me things aren't working. We try to reassure grantees that we're not going to judge them or punish them for disappointing results, and that we all need to learn from things that don't work.*

I hear this sentiment over and over when I work with organizations and funders. Funders typically appreciate honesty, along with an action plan of how data will be used to improve. Innovation often requires failure, and your program is no different. For example, I worked with an organization long ago—the same one I talked about in Chapter 4, Build a Culture of Evaluation.

I emailed them the program evaluation report (rookie mistake, don't do that), and was excited to meet with them the next day to discuss. Before I arrived, I received a call from my client: "The data are wrong."

I thought to myself, what could they be talking about?

He went on to explain. "The data are wrong. The report says everyone said our communication is poor, but it's not. We email them, and we do communicate. We can't send this to our funder." I agreed to listen and discuss when I arrived.

I really pondered this. The report was overall very positive, yet they chose to focus on this one small piece where the data showed something negative. I recognized their attachment to the work going well as well as the fear that the funder might pull their money. I quickly sketched an improvement plan based on the data.

When we met, I calmly shared that while they may have felt the data were wrong, it's what their participants feel. It's not the data that were wrong, it's that they needed to change how they were communicating. This brought a sigh of relief to all.

We worked through a one-page improvement plan, outlining how they would change their communication approach to include monthly phone calls, a Google forum for group discussion, as well as emails.

When we surveyed everyone again a few months later, the data showed communication was no longer an issue. The following year, the funder gave them even more money, saying that they appreciated the honesty and transparency, and how they used the data to improve their programs.

The point of this story? If you find something isn't working, get curious about how you can improve the program. What can you change based on the data? This is the essence of using data for program improvement, and it establishes your organization as a learning one.

## Use Data to Improve Program Implementation

Program evaluation is an organizational development tool, informing what's working and what is not working. This streamlines implementation, making the most of resources so they have the most impact. Put simply: evaluation helps you get more bang for the buck.

Your program evaluation process needs to fit your organization. Whether you gather data on an ongoing basis to inform program activities or annually to understand overall operations, the data provide you with a map to make informed decisions, taking the guesswork out of which program activities you should or shouldn't do.

### Example: Program improvement based on evaluation data (NHA)

NW Housing Alternatives implemented its program evaluation system alongside a new database solution. The combination of these efforts allowed them to track data and access reports to improve programs on an ongoing basis.

The paper "Program Evaluation and Data Culture in Resident Services" by Julia Doty and myself describes how their program planning efforts went from being reactive to proactive:

*The use of a new Housing Stability Assessment was developed as a part of the program evaluation system. We offer specific services and resources that help the household stabilize, avoid eviction, and/or access opportunities for growth. Before program evaluation, our intervention strategy was to have a resident household approach them with a need. Now, we use data to distill available resources to focus on just those which are most applicable and helpful to that specific household.*

Julia shared how their data culture has transformed as a result of program evaluation.

*Data culture for our team includes using a lens of evaluation when making modifications to our program, ensuring that it is part of the process every step of the way. We do not use data to prove that we are doing everything right; rather, we utilize data from our program to continually improve, knowing that some interventions will be more successful than others.*

*For instance, we recently implemented a new move-in assessment which allows residents to identify areas in which they need assistance. The purpose of this tool is both to improve program orientation for residents, as well as offer an opportunity to stabilize households directly after move-in. Creation of this tool was based on recent survey data that showed that there was a lack of understanding of what our program offered. However, we know we can't implement a new intervention without simultaneously creating a way to assess its impact. We built a tracking mechanism into our database, and over time we will assess whether the tool has achieved its two main goals based on utilization and future surveying. In this way, data culture for our team has brought us to a consistent lens of measurement and effectiveness in our operations.*

## Example: Program improvement based on evaluation data (Special Olympics Oregon)

Special Olympics Oregon wanted to set up a program evaluation process for its Unified Champion Schools program (formerly Project Unify). The program goals were:

*To use sports as a catalyst to foster respect, dignity, and advocacy for people with intellectual disabilities (ID).*

*To create opportunities for young people to promote respect, dignity, and advocacy for people with ID.*

We gathered data from student participants with and without ID, parents, teachers, and principals. Here's what we found in the year one report, and how data were used to improve the program.

*The Year One report showed school liaisons felt communications could be improved between our staff and themselves. The original program model included a county-based volunteer who communicated with the schools within their county as well as to our program staff at the state level. Volunteers are doing the job on weekends, evenings, and school staff communicated during the school day.*

*Since communication was reported as a challenge, we removed the volunteers and had school liaisons communicate directly with staff at the state level, taking out the middle person. We also created a Unified Champion Schools Playbook that outlined how to implement the program from beginning to end. We provided trainings for all school liaisons, and then they kept the playbook for future reference.*

As a result, communications improved and increased the number of schools we could serve.

## Use Data to Show Impact

Showing impact is a critical use of data: informing staff, board, funders, and the community at large on the difference your program makes.

A realistic and meaningful program evaluation system provides a clear path to gather your data and compile them into meaningful reports. Different organizations leverage these reports in different ways to illustrate impact. You can distribute the impact summary report through your website, newsletter, and other marketing methods. You can also share points from the Program Impact Summary report at a fundraising event.

Being able to share the impact you made is critical for fundraising, marketing, and communications efforts. Data can help you tell your story in meaningful and effective ways to illustrate what you do and the difference your program makes.

### Example: Show impact through data (PHFS)

Portland Homeless Family Solutions (PHFS) experienced a transformation by using evaluation findings to illustrate impact. Before implementing a program evaluation system, they had little data on impact to share with funders, and their grant acceptance rate was low.

Their program evaluation system provided data that demonstrated their impact on families. Now their grant acceptance rate is around 90 percent. Before, PHFS did not do annual reports. Now it's a regular part of their annual activities. As Brandi Tuck,

Executive Director of Portland Homeless Family Solutions, shared:

*Reporting to funders changed as a result of implementing a program evaluation system. It's no coincidence because we have a straightforward evaluation design. In all of these grants, we include our five outcomes. We almost always get the grants because we have the metrics so we can show what we are doing. Our fundraising philosophy is based on Penelope Burke's work, 'Donors want to see the impact their dollars are having in the community.' We give them our annual report. It's straightforward, and it's easy for donors to understand the impact.*

*So many organizations are doing great work, and don't have fundraising success we have because they cannot show their impact in a clear and concise manner. What surprised me about the evaluation design is how easy it was. We got everyone together. It was very simple. People think evaluation is going to be some big scary process that requires some statistical analysis and a high level of expertise, and it doesn't.*

I have enjoyed hearing stories like this many times over the years. Once you have the data, you can demonstrate your impact. Once you can demonstrate your impact, funders are more likely to be interested in supporting your program.

# Final Thoughts

Here are some resources to continue building your program evaluation muscles:

The companion website 💻: www.evaluationintoaction.com/getyourdata has examples and information to support you through your program evaluation journey.

**Evaluation into Action** (www.evaluationintoaction.com) has resources to further your education, a blog with evaluation insights, and a quarterly newsletter filled with information, events, and more. We also provide coaching, training, and a range of program evaluation services.

**American Evaluation Association** (www.eval.org) offers many webinars, conferences, and other educational opportunities. With local affiliates throughout the United States, there's probably one in your area, so check it out.

Thank you for making the journey through this book! Program evaluation is an empowering tool. Finding what works for your organization is the key to unlocking the potential of what data can do for you. Regardless of your expertise or organization size, the path of program evaluation is there for you to get the data you need to improve programs and show impact.

If you need help along the way, visit www.evaluationintoaction.com for training and coaching programs designed to meet you wherever you're at. I am passionate about making program evaluation accessible to all.

# References

Joan Garry Consulting. 2017. "14 Attributes of a Thriving Nonprofit." *Title of the blog.* https://blog.joangarry.com/best-non-profit-organizations/ January 18, 2017.

Evaluation Mini-Guide #2: *Measurement Methods and Tools.* 2014. Kelly Jarvis, NPC Research and Chari Smith, Evaluation into Action (formerly CRSmith Consulting). A resource funded by the Oregon Arts Commission for the Connecting students to the World of Work grantees.

Hutchinson, Kylie. 2016. *Survive and thrive: Three steps to securing your program's sustainability.* Vancouver, BC: Community Solutions.

Dr. Patton, Michael Quinn. 1997. *Utilization-focused evaluation.* Thousand Oaks, CA: Sage.

Deussen, Dr. Theresa and Nelsestuen, Kari. "Being a Savvy Consumer of Evaluation. Education Now and in the Future Conference." Portland, Oregon. February 10, 2004. Northwest Regional Educational Laboratory.

Kanter, Beth and Sherman, Aliza. 2017. *Happy Healthy Nonprofit.* Wiley Publishing.

Trochim, William M.K. 2006. *Research Methods Knowledge Base.* Web Center for Social Research Methods.

Germann, P. J. "Development of the Attitude toward Science in School Assessment and Its Use to Investigate the Relationship between Science Achievement and Attitude toward Science in School," *Journal of Research in Science Teaching* 25 (1988), 680–703.

W.K. Kellogg Foundation. 2004. *The Logic Model Development Guide.* https://www.bttop.org/sites/default/files/public/W.K.%20 Kellogg%20LogicModel.pdf

Jones, Sheri Chaney. 2014. "Outputs vs. Outcomes Matters." Measurement Resources Blog. February 2, 2014.

Dr. Evergreen, Stephanie. 2017. *Presenting Data Effectively.* Thousand Oaks, CA: Sage.

Evaluation Mini-Guide #2. *Measurement Methods and Tools.* 2014. Kelly Jarvis, NPC Research and Chari Smith, Evaluation into Action (formerly CRSmith Consulting). A resource funded by the Oregon Arts Commission for the Connecting students to the World of Work grantees.

McCubbin, H. I., McCubbin, M. A., Patterson, J. M., Cauble, A. E., Wilson, L. R., and Warwick, W. 1983. CHIP-Coping Health Inventory for Parents: An Assessment of Parental Coping Patterns in the Care of the Chronically Ill Child. *Journal of Marriage and Family*, May, 359-370.

Dr. Robinson, Sheila and Dr. Firth Leonard, Kim. 2018. *Designing Quality Survey Questions.* Thousand Oaks, CA: Sage.

Evaluation Mini-Guide #3: *Permissions and Confidentiality 2014* Kelly Jarvis, NPC Research and Chari Smith, Evaluation into Action (formerly CRSmith Consulting). A resource funded by the Oregon Arts Commission for the Connecting students to the World of Work grantees.

Evaluation Mini-Guide #4: *Data Collection.* 2014. Kelly Jarvis, NPC Research and Chari Smith, Evaluation into Action (formerly CRSmith Consulting). A resource funded by the Oregon Arts Commission for the Connecting students to the World of Work grantees.

Evaluation Mini-Guide #5: *Data Management*. 2014. Kelly Jarvis, NPC Research and Chari Smith, Evaluation into Action (formerly CRSmith Consulting). A resource funded by the Oregon Arts Commission for the Connecting students to the World of Work grantees.

Dr. Patton, Michael Quinn. 2012. *Essentials of Utilization-Focused Evaluation*. Thousands Oaks, CA, Sage. (p. 4)

Made in the USA
Las Vegas, NV
18 December 2023

83048544R00138